THE IMPORTANCE OF

H.G. Wells

by
Don Nardo

Lucent Books, P.O. Box 289011, San Diego, CA 92198-9011

These and other titles are included in The Importance Of biography series:

Benjamin Franklin
Chief Joseph
Christopher Columbus
Marie Curie
Galileo Galilei
Richard M. Nixon
Jackie Robinson
H.G. Wells

Library of Congress Cataloging-in-Publication Data

Nardo, Don, 1947–
    H.G. Wells / by Don Nardo
    p. cm.—(The Importance of)
    Includes bibliographical references and index.
Summary: Explores the life of the wide-ranging British author known for his science fiction, histories, and novels and discusses his efforts to achieve social change through his books.
    ISBN 1-56006-025-5
    1. Wells, H.G. (Herbert George), 1866–1946—Juvenile literature. 2. Novelists, English—20th century—Biography—Juvenile literature. 3. Science fiction, English—History and criticism—Juvenile literature. 4. Social problems in litera-ture—Juvenile literature. [1. Wells, H.G. (Herbert George), 1866–1946. 2. Authors, English.]
    I. Title. II. Series.
PR5776.N37   1992
823'.912—dc20   92-19870
[B]   CIP
                                                                  AC

Contents

Foreword

THE IMPORTANCE OF biography series deals with individuals who have made a unique contribution to history. The editors of the series have deliberately chosen to cast a wide net and include people from all fields of endeavor. Individuals from politics, music, art, literature, philosophy, science, sports, and religion are all represented. In addition, the editors did not restrict the series to individuals whose accomplishments have helped change the course of history. Of necessity, this criterion would have eliminated many whose contribution was great, though limited. Charles Darwin, for example, was responsible for radically altering the scientific view of the natural history of the world. His achievements continue to impact the study of science today. Others, such as Chief Joseph of the Nez Percé, played a pivotal role in the history of their own people. While Joseph's influence does not extend much beyond the Nez Percé, his nonviolent resistance to white expansion and his continuing role in protecting his tribe and his homeland remain an inspiration to all.

These biographies are more than factual chronicles. Each volume attempts to emphasize an individual's contributions both in his or her own time and for posterity. For example, the voyages of Christopher Columbus opened the way to European colonization of the New World. Unquestionably, his encounter with the New World brought monumental changes to both Europe and the Americas in his day. Today, however, the broader impact of Columbus's voyages is being critically scrutinized. *Christopher Columbus,* as well as every biography in The Importance Of series, includes and evaluates the most recent scholarship available on each subject.

Each author includes a wide variety of primary and secondary source quotations to document and substantiate his or her work. All quotes are footnoted to show readers exactly how and where biographers derive their information, as well as provide stepping stones to further research. These quotations enliven the text by giving readers eyewitness views of the life and times of each individual covered in The Importance Of series.

Finally, each volume is enhanced by photographs, bibliographies, chronologies, and comprehensive indexes. For both the casual reader and the student engaged in research, The Importance Of biographies will be a fascinating adventure into the lives of people who have helped shape humanity's past, present, and will continue to shape its future.

Important Dates in the Life of H.G. Wells

Wells is born in Bromley, — **1866**
a town near London.

1884 — Attends London University and
studies under T.H. Huxley.

Sells his first piece of
writing—"The Rediscovery — **1891**
of the Unique."

Weds Amy Robbins, whom
1894 — he calls Jane; they begin
living together.

Publishes *The Time Machine*, — **1895**
establishes self as an
important writer.

1898 — Publishes *The War of the Worlds*.

1901

Builds and moves into Spade — **1903** — Son Frank is born.
House in Sandgate with Jane;
publishes *Anticipations*, first — **1905**
utopian work; son Gip is born.

1909 — Publishes *Tono-Bungay* and
Publishes *Kipps*. — *Ann Veronica;* latter creates a
public scandal.

Publishes *The Outline of History*; — **1920**
establishes self as historian.

1927 — Jane dies of cancer.

Publishes autobiography. — **1934**

1939 — Publishes *The Fate of Homo
Sapiens* and *The New World
Order.*

Wells dies in sleep. — **1946**

The World Builder

When most people hear the name H.G. Wells, they think of the fantastic characters and events he created in his novels. They think of Martians attacking the earth or time machines whisking people into bizarre and bleak environments. They picture the invisible man, his face wrapped in bandages. Or they envision scientists traveling in quaint craft to the moon and discovering life and other marvels beneath its dusty surface. People may also know of Wells as a great predictor who foretold the coming of new gadgets and technologies long before their actual invention. All of these colorful images are indeed part of Wells' legacy. He was a man who used his powerful imagination and writing talent to shape strange and fascinating worlds.

But Wells did much more than create imaginary and future societies for people's entertainment. He spent most of his time and considerable energies in an attempt to achieve what he believed was a much larger and more important goal. Wells took on the gigantic task of trying to restructure his own society and build a better world.

Like many people in the late 1800s and early 1900s, Wells was saddened and distressed by the amount of human misery around the globe. Seemingly senseless and avoidable wars regularly devastated whole countries. Powerful nations used their armies to colonize and exploit less developed peoples. Factories spewed black smoke and other wastes into the environment as the workers wasted away in crime-ridden slums. Though many people wanted to see these and other ills of society eliminated, they lacked the means or courage to work for change.

Wells felt that he could use his fame and talent as a writer to create change. He sincerely believed that, through his writings, he could stir people's hearts and inspire them to reform society. And he devoted his life to this aim. To carry out his purpose, in book after book, he created stories that exposed society's ills. Through his characters, he lectured, preached, and pleaded for people to end the miseries of the past. And he used words to paint vivid blueprints for building a more peaceful, equitable, and productive world. The scope of Wells' vision is reflected in the ambitious titles he chose: *New Worlds for Old*, *The World Set Free*, *The War That Will End War*, *The Fate of Homo Sapiens*, and *The New World Order*.

But the task Wells had taken upon himself was too large for any one person. He did succeed in making people think about their world. But they did not respond to his writing as he had intended—by clamoring for social reforms. His readers saw his works mainly as fascinating, imaginative entertainment, and that opinion remains his legacy. The consistent failure to stimulate social change perplexed and frustrated Wells all his life. He became what writer Alfred Borrello called an author in agony. But he never stopped trying. The story of H.G. Wells is the story of a man who, in the face of impossible odds, stubbornly refused to give up. It is the story of a man who imagined a better world, then tried to make that vision a reality.

Chapter

1 Escape from Childhood

On September 21, 1866, in Bromley, a small town on the outskirts of London, England, Joseph and Sarah Wells had their third son. They named him Herbert George but called him by the nickname Bertie until he was in his teens. Young Bertie's earliest impression of life was that it was a struggle. His rivalry with his older brothers, Frank and Fred, gave him his first taste of that struggle. "My childish relations with my brothers varied between vindictive [spiteful] resentment and . . . aggression," the grown-up H.G. Wells recalled. "I made a terrific fuss if my toys or games were touched. . . . I bit and scratched my brothers and I kicked their shins, because I was a sturdy little boy who had to defend himself."[1] The attempt to get along with his brothers occupied much of his time during his first few years.

Wells, an unusually perceptive child, became aware at an early age that his parents were also engaged in a struggle—a monthly battle to pay the bills. His father ran a tiny glass and china shop called Atlas House, located on Bromley's narrow main street. Sarah, his mother, worked part-time as a housemaid in elegant mansions in London and also helped run the shop. The family lived in a set of drab rooms behind and below the shop. The business was never successful, partly because Joseph

was lazy and had no interest in running it. He preferred drinking and playing cricket, a game similar to baseball, with his friends. He spent a great deal of time away from home, leaving Sarah alone to tend the shop, as well as raise the children and keep the house.

Another reason the business was unsuccessful was that it could not compete with larger china shops in nearby London. Many of the other businesses in Bromley

H.G. Wells at age ten. Wells, nicknamed Bertie by his parents, learned early that life was a struggle.

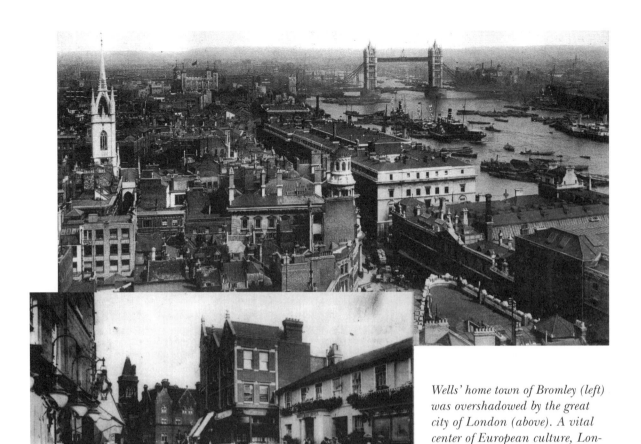

Wells' home town of Bromley (left) was overshadowed by the great city of London (above). A vital center of European culture, London deeply influenced Wells' early ideas and attitudes about life.

also eventually failed. Among them were Mr. Cooper's tailor shop next door to Atlas House and Percy Oliver's boot and shoe store across the street. While still very young, H.G. Wells learned that his town, like the family business, struggled to exist in the shadow of the ever-expanding city.

At the Hub of Western Society

London influenced Wells in other ways, too. His childhood so near this city had a crucial impact on the early development of his ideas and attitudes. At the time, London held more than three million people, nearly one-seventh the population of Great Britain. The city was the hub of the British Empire and one of the world's major centers of finance, industry, art, and learning. London stood, along with Paris, as one of the two great cultural pillars of Western, or European-based, society. It was significant that Wells grew up in the city that was the heart of British government, commerce, and social customs. From the time Bertie Wells could first speak, his mother and older brothers instilled in him

British customs, ideas, and values. Even before he was old enough to attend school, he believed there was something special about these ideas and values. He accepted the popular British notion that his country was more civilized than most other countries.

Wells grew up during the height of the Victorian era. In this period, marked by Queen Victoria's 1837–1901 reign, Great Britain was the most powerful country in the world. Britain had colonized lands on every continent. Contingents of the British army organized and controlled huge populations in India, Africa, and other regions, and the invincible British navy ruled the seas.

The vast trade network sustained by this great empire brought prosperity to many British citizens and supported the rapid growth of British industry. Most British people became confident that Britain's economic and military systems would continue to bring prosperity and order. Many believed that new ideas and inventions would also contribute to this prosperity and raise living standards. Thus, in the late 1800s, there was a feeling of optimism about the future, a belief that progress would bring prosperity. As a child, Wells shared this belief. The idea that economic and intellectual progress would bring about a better future later became a major theme of his writing.

A Frustrated Childhood

The rigid class structure of British society also strongly affected Wells' early childhood. This system determined people's worth as human beings by how much money they made, what work they did, and what families they were born into. It was not the government, but tradition, that imposed the class system. The people themselves perpetuated the system by accepting it as the "natural order" of everyday life. According to custom, each group in society had its function and rightful place in the order of things. Most people believed that maintaining their own positions on the social ladder helped keep society strong. Only rarely did people socialize or marry outside of their "stations" in life. Those who did usually encountered scorn or hostility, and found it difficult to fit in. The upper classes consisted mainly of the nobility, church and government leaders, and wealthy landowners. Most British people belonged to the middle and lower classes, which included small farmers, merchants, and laborers.

Queen Victoria ruled Great Britain for sixty-five years. Her long reign brought progress and prosperity to Britain. H.G. Wells, like most Britons of his time, believed progress was the key to a better future for all.

Wells' father, Joseph, was content with his drab, lower-class existence as a shopkeeper. His lack of ambition mystified young Bertie.

As small shopkeepers, Joseph and Sarah Wells were considered members of the lower-middle class. Like most people, they accepted their station, believing it to be part of the natural order, and did not aspire to higher positions on the social ladder. This attitude perplexed and bothered the young H.G. Wells. He could not understand why his parents and brothers so easily accepted living in Atlas House's small, colorless rooms. As the biographer Lovat Dickson put it, he was "plainly impatient with the . . . dumb acceptance of the order of things that held them all in that . . . [less than ideal] home."[2] Wells found it strange and frustrating that his parents did not long, as he did, for a better way of life. He did not yet understand that the Victorian optimism about working toward a more prosperous future was a feeling expressed mainly by people of the upper classes. The inequalities of the class system would later become a prominent theme in Wells' writings.

Another source of frustration for the young Wells was his mother's unhappiness. Because Joseph Wells so often left her alone with the duties of the shop, house, and children, Sarah felt abandoned and overworked. She deeply resented her husband for this, writing in her diary, "What happiness have I known as a wife? Morose [gloomy] unpleasant treatment shut in night after night *alone* . . . my children in bed and I left to work . . . woman is destined for man's *slave*."[3]

Wells often tried to relieve his mother of some of the household drudgery. At the age of seven, he spent much of his time helping her in the family's dingy, poorly lit basement kitchen below the shop. The shadows of customers and passersby flickered across a patch of light filtering through a small grating in the ceiling. Often, the boy felt deprived of the light of day and feared that he would be trapped in these surroundings for the rest of his life. Desperately, he longed to escape into a better world.

An Extraordinary Mind

To some degree, Bertie accomplished this goal by retreating into a world of books. In his imagination, he saw himself escaping from Bromley and traveling to other lands and other times. Wells later recalled discovering "the art of leaving my body to sit impassive [unmoving] in a crumpled-up attitude [position] in a chair or sofa, while I wandered over the hills and far away in novel company and new scenes."[4] He was so bright that, even at the age of seven, he read faster and remembered more of what he read than did most adults. Lovat Dickson described him as a "pale under-sized little boy, with bold eyes, very blue in colour . . . reading in that dim [kitchen] light books borrowed from the local library. . . . [The miracle of blind] chance had produced in this youngest son of almost uneducated parents a child with an extraordinary mind, possessed of amazing powers of memorization and a brilliant imagination."[5]

Wells began to express his imagination by dreaming up elaborate and vivid fantasies. He usually pictured himself as a great and noble military general at the command of an invincible army. The general's goal was to destroy the forces that enslaved humanity. Wells later recalled:

I used to walk about Bromley, a small rather undernourished boy, meanly clad [poorly clothed] and whistling detestably [badly] between his teeth, and no one suspected that a phantom staff [of generals] pranced about me and phantom orderlies [soldiers] galloped at my commands, to shift the guns and concentrate fire on those houses below, to launch the final attack on yonder distant ridge. . . . Martin's Hill [near his home] is indeed one of the great battlegrounds of history. . . . I and my cavalry swept the broken masses [armies] away towards Croydon [a neighboring village], pressed them ruthlessly through a night of slaughter on to the pitiful surrender of the remnant at dawn . . . kings and presidents, and the great of the earth, came to salute my saving wisdom. I was simple even in victory. I made wise and firm decisions, about morals and customs . . . [6]

Wells' mental gifts and reading ability gave him an advantage few other children at the time possessed—the power to educate himself. He realized early that, in order to break free of the lower-class life he hated, a good education was essential. But he also found that there was little to be learned at school. As the biographer Norman Mackenzie commented, "England at that time was poorly served by its schools, which at all levels were badly equipped, badly run and hopelessly inadequate."[7] A

Bromley's town hall was the center of public life. The larger world of nearby London, however, held a stronger attraction for Wells.

few of the wealthier schools, maintained and attended by members of the upper classes, offered decent education and had international reputations. But most British schools, like the one Wells first attended, could not afford well-educated teachers. So the general state of British education was dismal.

To further his own learning, the boy read hundreds of adult-level books before he was fourteen. Among his favorites were Jonathan Swift's *Gulliver's Travels,* Tom Paine's *Common Sense,* and Plato's *Republic.* All of these works criticized the society their authors lived in and offered formulas for constructing better, more ordered societies. In these books, the new societies were always ruled by people of unusually great intelligence. The ideas that Wells acquired from these books in this early stage of his life stayed with him. As he grew older, he

Plato described his vision of the ideal state in Republic. *The book had a lasting influence on Wells, who read it while he was still a young boy.*

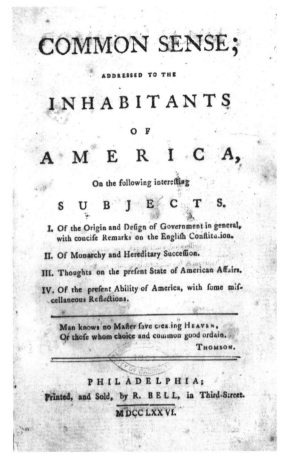

COMMON SENSE;

ADDRESSED TO THE

INHABITANTS

OF

AMERICA,

On the following interesting

SUBJECTS.

I. Of the Origin and Design of Government in general, with concise Remarks on the English Constitution.

II. Of Monarchy and Hereditary Succession.

III. Thoughts on the present State of American Affairs.

IV. Of the present Ability of America, with some miscellaneous Reflections.

Man knows no Master save creaing HEAVEN, Or those whom choice and common good ordain.

THOMSON.

PHILADELPHIA;

Printed, and Sold, by R. BELL, in Third-Street.

MDCCLXXVI.

The title page from Thomas Paine's famous political work Common Sense. *Paine's ideas helped shape Wells' own thinking.*

thought more and more about the possibility of shaping a better world. And as an adult, he would devote much of his time and energy to achieving this lofty goal.

Feeling Imprisoned

The routine of Wells' life changed abruptly in 1880, when he was fourteen. Although there was no official divorce, his mother finally decided to leave his father. She found a full-time job as a live-in maid at

Up Park, a large mansion in Sussex, a few miles south of London. Frank and Fred had already left home, so she had only the welfare of her youngest son to consider. Unable to bring him with her to Up Park, she found Bertie a position as an apprentice to a draper, or cloth dealer.

But young Wells had no desire to learn draping or any other trade, and he was miserable. He had to work seventy hours a week and received only a bit of pocket money in exchange. On July 4, 1880, in a letter to his mother, he described his boring daily routine:

> Here I am, sitting in my bedroom after the fatigues of the day etc. Cough slightly better & I am tolerably [just barely] comfortable. Morning: we sleep 4 together every 3 apprentices & 1 of the hands [assistants] in one room (of course in separate beds). We lay in bed until 7:30 when a bell rings & we jump up & put trousers slippers socks & jacket on over nightgown & hurry down & dust the shop etc. About 8:15 we hurry upstairs & dress & wash for breakfast. At 8:30 we go into a sort of vault underground (lit by gas) & have breakfast. After breakfast I am in the shop & desk till dinner at 1 (we have dinner underground as well as breakfasts) & then work till tea (which we have in the same place) & then go on to supper at 8:30 at which time work is done & we may then go out until 10:30 at which hour the apprentices are obliged to be in the house. I don't like the place much . . .[8]

The boy later commented that, during this time, he felt as if he were trapped inside a great machine from which escape was impossible.

Wells' mother, Sarah, left his father when Wells was fourteen. Wells moved in with her a few months later. Her bleak existence as a chambermaid made a lasting impression on the youth.

But escape came quickly. Wells' employers saw his lack of interest and dismissed him after three months. Sarah begged her employer to allow the boy to live at Up Park and he moved into a tiny attic room. There, he spent much of his time reading. His mother lived in two small, poorly lit basement rooms that reminded him of the kitchen at Atlas House and the eating room below the draper's shop. Many other aspects of life at Up Park revolved around the underground. Wells often watched Sarah hurry to and fro through a maze of underground tunnels. These linked Up Park's servants' quarters to the kitchen and other work areas. The continuous succession of dingy cellars and tunnels of his boyhood became powerful images in Wells' mind. He saw these underground chambers as symbols of the bleak, miserable lives of the working classes. He would later explore the dark side of living underground in some of his greatest novels.

Another aspect of the labors of the working classes that Wells noticed at this time was the factory system. Although he did not work in a factory, he often watched the industrial workers going to and from work. And he heard firsthand accounts of life in the factories from workers who associated with the servants he knew at Up Park. He learned how the machines and factories of the Industrial Revolution were changing society. Before the age of machines in the early 1800s, England had consisted mostly of picturesque countryside dotted with farms and quaint villages.

There had been only a few large towns and cities. Then the building of factories drew millions of people away from the land in search of manufacturing jobs. New jobs and large numbers of manufactured products helped increase the prosperity of the country. But there were drawbacks to the system. As the cities grew, cheap slums grew up around the factories to house the workers. These areas often became rat-infested, garbage-ridden havens for disease, crime, and despair. "Rural England had become the world that was lost," explains Norman Mackenzie. "And for millions the green fields beyond the smoke [of the factories] were soon to be little more than a nostalgic memory."[9] These ills of industrial society would later become powerful images in many of Wells' writings.

Life in the Drapery Shop

As a teenager, Wells worked in a drapery shop, a job he hated. He longed to become a teacher, and, on July 10, 1880, in a moment of depression, penned an emotional letter to his mother begging her to let him quit.

"Time here is wasted. I cannot study here in a room crowded with a set of noisy lads after twelve hours misery [working in the shop]. . . . A month lost, absolutely lost now only means another month added on to the time I am to be a clog [weight] around your neck. . . . I have been so foolish as to waste the greater part of 17 years, more than ¼ of my life already. . . . I have a fearful lot of leeway to make up & must get to work [teaching] at once if you will let me. I shall set a small value on my life, the fag End of my life [old age], I shall not enjoy it very much if I have to look back not on a success & well-earned rewards, but on so much time spent on half-hearted work. . . . It would be the kindest & wisest thing you could do now to let me leave here very soon."

The Industrial Revolution changed England from a rural, agriculturally based society into an urban manufacturing center. The ills of industrial society later became topics in Wells' writings.

A Fascination with Science

Because his reading ability and powers of perception were well beyond his years, even as a teenager Wells saw more in the factory system than manufactured products and slums. He realized, as few adults did, that the machines and inventions of science were the driving force behind the growth of industry. Science had also brought about increasingly efficient weapons of war such as the submarine and machine gun, which came into use in the 1880s. Thus, the young Wells formed the strong impression that science could, if handled unwisely, cause much unhappiness. At the same time, he saw that science also brought many benefits to humanity. These included better ways to communicate, like the telegraph, more advanced farming techniques, and new ways to fight disease. It became clear to Wells that science had a dual nature, one that had the potential for both good and evil. Fascinated by all aspects of science, he began to read every science book he could get his hands on. By the time he was fifteen, he had decided to become a science teacher.

With this goal in mind, Wells studied hard in the Sussex school he attended while living at Up Park. It was much better than most other schools of the day, thanks to the abilities of the headmaster, Horace Byatt. Byatt immediately saw that Wells had a remarkable mind and took a keen interest in him. In 1883, when Wells was only seventeen, Byatt invited him to become an

Slums spread as nineteenth-century England industrialized. Wells compared the drudgery of working-class life to being trapped in a great machine.

assistant teacher. For several months, Wells taught science in the daytime and studied more advanced material with Byatt at night. Eagerly, the young man crammed his mind with the latest knowledge about astronomy, chemistry, geology, and mathematics. In 1884, Byatt offered Wells a full-time position in his school. But by this time, Wells had bigger plans. He politely turned down the offer, informing Byatt that he had earned a scholarship to attend London University. Because he had scored well on a government-sponsored exam, all of his expenses would be paid.

Wells looked forward to attending the university because of its growing reputation as one of the best colleges in the

world. He was especially eager to study with one particular teacher at the school, Thomas H. Huxley, who was renowned as one of the greatest scientists of the day. Huxley had earned the nickname "Darwin's bulldog" because he championed biologist Charles Darwin's ideas about evolution. This doctrine holds that, over the course of millions of years, all living things undergo physical change. Darwin said that modern advanced life forms descended from lower, less complex forms. When this idea appeared six years before Wells' birth, it caused much controversy because it seemed to contradict the biblical explanation of creation—that God made all creatures in finished form in a

few days. But, thanks in great part to the efforts of Huxley, by the 1880s nearly all reputable scientists had accepted the theory of evolution. The basic idea has since remained controversial only in nonscientific circles.

Wells studied biology under Huxley for only a year. But in that short time both Huxley the man and Huxley's ideas on evolution had a profound effect on Wells. Huxley, an imposing figure with a great mane of white hair and an air of complete authority, seemed almost godlike to Wells. "I believed then he was the greatest man I

Thomas Huxley, one of England's greatest minds, taught Wells biology at London University. Wells believed Huxley was the greatest man he had ever met. Wells' intelligence and learning so impressed his teacher at this Sussex grammar school that he was made assistant teacher.

Wells Lands a Teaching Job

Wells' mother allowed him to leave the drapery shop. He soon landed a position as an assistant teacher at a Sussex school run by Horace Byatt. In his book H.G. Wells, *biographer Lovat Dickson describes how the boy tried to make up for lost time.*

"So he was released and became an under-master at the age of seventeen in the little two-roomed grammar school that stood opposite the great gates of Cowdray Park in Sussex. The earnest youth in the cheap, ready-made clothes, wearing in his rambles around the countryside as well as in the town and at school the mortarboard [flat cap with tassel attached] which signified his association with the profession of teaching, suddenly found himself happier than he had ever dreamed would be possible. The years of intellectual starvation had left him with such an appetite for learning that he felt he could never read enough. In order to make up for lost time, he vowed not to read any novels or to play any games. He and the other assistant master, Harris, shared rooms over a little confectionary [candy and pastry] shop in the High Street, rooms hung with encouraging slogans . . . very much like the room with its slanting ceiling, its lead-framed, diamond-paned dormer window, its bulging walls and its view of the vicarage garden, described in *Love and Mr. Lewisham* [a novel Wells wrote as an adult]."

was ever likely to meet," Wells wrote at the age of sixty-eight. "And I believe that all the more firmly today. The year I spent in Huxley's class was, beyond all question, the most educational year of my life."[10]

Wells found, to his delight, that Huxley shared his belief in the dual nature of science. Huxley preached that the development of science had occurred when the human brain had evolved to a certain level of complexity. If used wisely, Huxley said, the marvels of science would allow civilization to reach new heights and humanity to evolve even farther. But, he warned, humans had begun as lowly creatures and still had a primitive side to their nature. Motivated by this dark side, people could conceivably use science to enslave others and manufacture weapons of destruction. Thus, Huxley reinforced Wells' idea that humanity was destined either to progress or to decline, depending on how people used the inventions of science. The use of science, for either good or ill, later became the central theme of many of Wells' greatest writings.

Thomas Huxley's ideas about Charles Darwin's (above) theory of evolution inspired Wells to begin writing stories.

A Vision of the Future

Wells' first significant strivings as a writer were inspired by Huxley's ideas about evolution. Huxley had suggested that humans would continue to evolve and change in the future. This made Wells wonder what a human being of the future would be like.

He concluded that "unless the order of the universe has come to an end, [man] will undergo further modification . . . and at last cease to be man, giving rise to some other type of animated [living] being."[11] Wells envisioned humans of the far future as having huge brains and shrunken bodies. He saw them floating in tubs of liquid nutrients under a great crystal dome. After destroying all other plants and animals on earth, he suggested, people might learn to absorb chemicals and sunlight as plants do today. Wells wanted to share this vision with others and decided the best way was to turn it into a descriptive story. He titled it "The Man of the Year Million," and circulated it to friends and classmates.

The tale received a great deal of praise and Wells realized that he had a talent for storytelling. Writing began to take up more and more of his spare time and he started thinking about the possibility of making a living as a writer. At the time, Wells did not dream that he would later become an author of worldwide fame and influence. What seemed important was that he had found a way to express his vivid imagination and, at the same time, make people think. He was still a long way from being a professional writer. But he felt that he had finally escaped from the worrisome, uncertain days of his childhood. He had discovered what might eventually be a path to a better and brighter future.

2 Travels in Time

The ten years following H.G. Wells' enrollment in London University in September 1884 were among the most important and turbulent in his life. During this period, he

Wells, as a student, poses in the biology lab as if contemplating humanity's evolution from the apes. The idea of humanity's continuing evolution greatly intrigued him.

studied under T.H. Huxley, taught children the marvels of science, and read constantly. All of these activities helped shape the ideas and personal attitudes that he would carry with him for the rest of his life. Also during these formative years, he made the decision to become a professional writer. Through hard work, he found a way to market his talent and establish himself as one of the most inventive writers of his day. At the same time, Wells' private life became more complicated. He overcame serious illness and depression, married twice, and began to support a household. These years marked his transformation from a student who was unsure of his future into a mature and successful adult writer.

Illness and Depression

Wells' interest in writing, which began in 1885 when he was still a student at the university, soon became a passion. After letting his classmates read his first story, "The Man of the Year Million," he published it in a newspaper called the *Science Schools Journal.* He continued to dabble in writing in his spare time and published another story in the *Journal* about a year later. Titled "A Tale of the Twentieth Century," it is about an advanced energy-producing machine that greatly modernizes the trains of the London subway system. "A Vision of the Past," about primitive humans, and "The Chronic Argonauts," about a man who travels into the future, soon followed. Although writing appealed to Wells, he was not sure that his stories were good enough to sell. Nor did he have any idea how to go about selling them. For a few years, the idea of a writing career remained a dream and, to earn a living, he pursued a career in teaching.

The first teaching job Wells landed after leaving London University in 1887 was at Holt Academy, a small boys' school in North Wales, about 170 miles northwest of London. Wells was immediately disappointed with the school and became depressed. In a letter to a friend, he wrote, "I wish I was dead. The boys are foolish & undisciplined to an astonishing degree. . . . There is an . . . utter absence of coherent [ordered] system in the whole damned affair."[12] One month after taking the job, Wells was thinking about quitting when a twist of fate made that option unnecessary. While playing football with the boys, he suffered a serious injury. He began coughing up blood and the local doctor diagnosed a crushed kidney. Other doctors disagreed, and Wells never knew the true nature of the physical problem that would periodically plague him for the rest of his life.

Late in 1887, at the age of twenty-one, Wells moved back in with his mother at Up Park to recover from his injury. At first, he feared he might be a permanent invalid, trapped in the dingy cellars of Up Park forever. Writing to a college friend, he jokingly called the place the House of the Captivity: Valley of the Shadow of Death.

Up Park, the estate where Wells' mother lived and worked. Wells also lived here before entering college and later returned to recover from a football injury.

He followed this with the mock newspaper headlines: "Illness of Wells! Thrilling Details! A Pint of Piddle [urine sample] Sent to London!"[13] But sometimes, his humor gave way to depression. He ended a letter to another friend with the words "Damn, damn, damn, damn, damn, damn, God damn, God damn, God damn, God damn."[14]

A New Beginning

By September 1888, Wells' health had improved and his depression had passed. He decided to stop feeling sorry for himself and start thinking more positively about his future. In another letter to a friend, he declared that he was no longer an invalid and that he had decided once more to pursue his career as a teacher.

During the next three years, Wells took several teaching jobs, including one at a boys' school run by John Vine Milne, the father of A.A. Milne, the creator of the literary character Winnie the Pooh. One of

Wells' students later described Wells at the age of twenty-three as

> somewhat below average height, not very robust in health, with evident signs of poverty, or at least . . . [without] any outward appearance of affluence. In dress, speech and manner he was plain and unvarnished [simple], abrupt and direct, with a somewhat cynical [critical] and outspoken scorn of the easy luxurious life of those who have obtained . . . social position or wealth. . . . He lectured for an hour each morning, and this was followed by a period of two hours in a laboratory, when he came round to each student in turn to explain and correct his dissections [of animals]. . . . He was extremely painstaking and evidently anxious to help each student. . . . He insisted that education consisted in the ability to . . . [tell the difference] between things of real importance and those of secondary or trivial import. . . . There was a real kindness and sympathy toward his pupils, many of whom were struggling against poverty and disadvantage.[15]

Most who knew Wells at this time agreed that he was an excellent teacher who cared deeply about the welfare of his students.

While earning a meager living teaching, Wells continued to write. In 1891, he penned an article titled "The Rediscovery of the Unique." It marked an important turning point in his life. In this article, he predicted that, although science would continue to expand humanity's knowledge, it would also reveal to people how much more there was to learn. Beyond the realm of human knowledge, he said, is the darkness of the unknown. Hidden in this darkness are the strange and fabulous secrets of the universe and creation. No matter how much people learn, suggested Wells, there will always be more secrets beyond their reach. He expressed this idea in the article's last paragraph, likening humanity to a man alone in darkness:

> Science is a match that man has just got alight. He thought he was in a room . . . and that his light would be reflected from and display walls inscribed with wonderful secrets and pillars carved with . . . [great knowledge]. It is a curious sensation now that the . . . flame burns up clear, to see his hands lit and just a glimpse of himself and the patch he stands on visible, and around him, in place of all that human comfort and beauty he anticipated—darkness still.[16]

In this single paragraph, Wells had expressed a theme on which many of his most famous works would be based. In both stories and novels, he would later use his imagination to conjure up some of the "wonderful secrets" from the darkness. He would create characters, often scientists, who would discover some of these secrets. And he would describe their despair at finding that their newfound knowledge was incomplete, useless, or even dangerous.

Wells thought the article was the best thing he had written to date. He got up his nerve and submitted the article to a famous and respected magazine, the *Fortnightly Review,* which was edited by the well-known journalist Frank Harris. To the young man's great surprise, Harris accepted the article and published it in July 1891. Wells made very little money from the sale, but he did not care. He had finally proven to himself that his dream of making a living writing might become a reality. It was a modest beginning, but a beginning nonetheless.

Isabel and Jane

While he was waiting for word from Harris about publication of "The Rediscovery of the Unique," Wells began spending a great deal of time with his cousin, Isabel Wells. They had dated off and on since 1887, but the relationship did not become serious until early in 1891. Wells described Isabel as

Amy Robbins, one of Wells' students, became the object of his affection in 1892. Unlike his wife, Robbins shared his scientific and literary interests.

Wells' cousin Isabel became his first wife on October 31, 1891. The couple soon discovered, however, that they wanted different things from life and the marriage ended.

a dark-eyed young woman with "a grave and lovely face, very firmly modelled, broad brows and a particularly beautiful mouth and chin and neck."[17] Though physically beautiful, Isabel was shy and unworldly and lacked Wells' intelligence and education. Most of the time, she listened politely as he talked incessantly about science, politics, and other topics she knew little about. He assumed she understood and agreed with his ideas. She assumed he wanted to settle down and lead a quiet life with her. Thinking they were in love, they married on October 31, 1891. They rented a house in Wandsworth, then a suburb of London.

Only a few weeks after they were married, both Wells and Isabel realized that they had made a mistake. Once they began living together, he learned that she did not share his interests after all. She often changed the subject or argued with him when he began a serious discussion. She, on the other hand, felt that he was self-centered and wanted to talk only about the subjects that interested him. Isabel was also disappointed that Wells

First Marriage a Mistake

Realizing that he had made a mistake in marrying his cousin Isabel and also that he was in love with Amy Robbins, Wells described the impending breakup of his marriage in a letter to friend Morley Davidson on December 27, 1893.

"I have been in very great trouble all of the past year—all the greater because it has been my own private affair. My own marriage has been a very great mistake. I love my wife very tenderly but not as a husband should love his wife, and—as quietly as possible—we are going to separate this New Year. . . . Our determination [to do so] has been our absolute secret until now. I shall get this house off my hands, and we shall return to different parts of London before the end of January. We are parting not in anger but in sorrow because our tempers, interests and desires are altogether different. . . . It is I that am doing this, and I am doing it because I love another woman with all my being."

refused to be content with teaching and earning a modest living. She was irritated with the extra time he put into writing, which she saw as the pursuit of an unrealistic dream. Though they were unhappy, they decided to stay together for the time being and make the best of things.

Wells' personal life became more complicated a few months later. Early in 1892, he became fascinated with one of his students, twenty-year-old Amy Robbins, who was studying to be a science teacher. Unlike Isabel, Amy shared Wells' interests. He and Amy became friends and frequently went to tea shops to talk. They fell in love. But because Wells was married, their relationship remained casual for almost two years. This situation changed when Wells and Isabel finally decided to separate in February 1894.

Immediately after the separation, Wells and Amy moved into an apartment together in another section of London. They spent many happy hours together, discussing science and taking long bicycle rides along London's Thames River. They gave each other pet names. He called her Jane, the name she used with almost everyone from that time on. She called him H.G., which became his most frequent nickname. Bright, charming, with a good sense of humor, she devoted herself to his happiness. Her understanding and loyalty would later help him through many of the personal and professional crises he would endure.

Finding a Market

It was during his last year of marriage to Isabel that Wells finally abandoned teaching and began to write for a living. In 1893,

Wells and Amy Robbins on the Thames River. The couple enjoyed bicycling together along the river and discussing science. It was Robbins who first called Wells "H.G.," the name by which he is best known.

he found a market for short articles in magazines like *Science and Art* and the popular *Pall Mall Gazette.* To his delight, after his first few sales, editors began asking him to submit more articles. He did not earn much per article but made up for it in the large number of articles that he wrote. Writing constantly and quickly, he turned out more than thirty articles by the end of 1893. In 1894, he published no fewer than seventy-five articles and five short stories.

Despite the large number of pieces he wrote, Wells' name was still not well known to the general public. Most literate people at the time read newspapers and books rather than magazines. But members of the publishing field began to notice him. One of his stories, "The Stolen Bacillus," caught the eye of W.E. Henley, the editor of the *National Observer.* This was one of the best and most widely read British newspapers of the day. Henley asked Wells to submit ideas for articles. Wells decided to dig up what he called his "peculiar treasure," "The Chronic Argonauts," his first published story about time travel, from the *Science Schools Journal.*

Over the years, Wells had revised "The Chronic Argonauts" several times. Now, he revised it again, expanding it into seven segments. Henley published these as a series of short episodes collectively titled "Time Traveler" over the course of four months in 1894. The editor received many favorable letters from his readers asking to see more stories about time travel. Henley himself found the pieces fresh and exciting and wanted to see the idea reach a wider audience. He arranged with a book publisher to publish a full-length book version of the series. In a letter, he urged Wells to take on the project, saying, "In your place I should go on [and write it]!. . . It [the idea] is so full of invention, & the invention is so wonderful . . . it must certainly make your reputation."[18]

By age twenty-nine, Wells had already published over a hundred articles and short stories. His huge literary output amazed his associates.

The Mysteries of Science

In their excellent biography of Wells, The Time Traveller: The Life of H.G. Wells, *Norman and Jeanne Mackenzie explain how Wells' first writing considered the nature of the unknown mysteries of science.*

"The significance of 'The Rediscovery of the Unique' lies in the fact that Wells was challenging both the optimism and the assumptions of science. Did the growth of science promise an unlimited extension of knowledge about Nature and Man's place in it—or did it merely demonstrate that the more that was known, the more plain it became that there were further unknowable mysteries? And was not science based on the belief that all phenomena were consistent and continuous, and therefore could be classified? Certainly that belief had permitted science to make great practical gains, because it allowed experiments to be repeated and the theoretical advances of physics and chemistry to be practically applied. But what if all units of matter were unique, and if the deviations from standardized [normal] behavior increased as the structures became more complicated, so that living organisms were more likely to behave in a unique fashion than aggregations [groupings] of molecules in a chemical compound, and Nature—the ultimate in complexity—might be quivering with uncertainties at which men could only guess?"

Success at Last

Wells jumped at the chance to write a novel. In only two weeks, he expanded and rewrote the "Time Traveler" series into a book, titling it *The Time Machine*. In this final version of the story, a scientist of the 1890s, referred to as the Time Traveler, invents a time machine. He journeys to the year 802,701 A.D. and finds that his own civilization has long since vanished. The earth is now inhabited by two races. Living above ground are the Eloi, childlike, irresponsible beings who are unable to even grow their own food. Living in underground tunnels are the Morlocks, half-animal creatures who mindlessly tend huge machines left from an earlier culture. They supply the Eloi with food and then prey upon them like cattle. The Time Traveler rescues a young Eloi girl from drowning and she becomes his companion as he explores the strange world of the future. Eventually, she disappears during a forest fire while he fights off an attack by dozens of Morlocks. After a brief journey to the still more distant future, the Time Traveler returns to his own time.

Appearing in bookstores in the summer of 1895, *The Time Machine* was an immediate success. Most critics raved about the book and called Wells a significant new voice in British literature. W.T. Stead of the *Review of Reviews* wrote, "H.G. Wells is a man of genius."[19] In the first five months, the book sold more than six thousand copies, at the time an unusually large number for a new author. Readers were fascinated by the idea of traveling through time, which no writer before had explored in such detail. And both the public and the critics found that Wells' vivid, highly descriptive writing style made the fantastic elements of the story (the parts based on fantasy about the future) seem very believable. A scene often praised in reviews was the one in which the Time Traveler briefly visits a desolate beach thirty million years in the future:

> At last, a steady twilight brooded over the earth, a twilight only broken now and then when a comet glared across the darkling sky. . . . All trace of the moon had vanished. . . . The sun, red and very large, halted motionless upon the horizon, a vast dome glowing with a dull heat. . . . The earth had come to rest with one face to the sun. . . . The sky was no longer blue . . . it was an inky black. . . . Far away up the desolate slope I heard a harsh scream and saw a thing like a huge white butterfly go slanting and fluttering up into the sky. . . . The sound of its voice was so dismal that I shivered and seated myself more firmly

upon the machine. Looking around me again, I saw that, quite near, what I had taken to be a reddish mass of rock was moving slowly towards me. Then I saw the thing was really a monstrous crablike creature. . . . I could see the many palps of its complicated mouth flickering and feeling as it moved.[20]

Ideas Frightening and Compelling

In addition to enjoying Wells' strong powers of description, readers and critics alike found the ideas in *The Time Machine* thought-provoking. Because of the poor state of education at the time, the reading public was relatively small. Most people who bought books were very well educated. They enjoyed and appreciated stories with underlying themes about popular ideas and institutions. Wells purposely aimed his writing at this perceptive audience. In the novel, he harshly criticized some of the social ills of his own time by using symbolic characters and places to represent Britain and its social classes. For example, Wells suggested that the beast-like Morlocks have evolved from the poor, uneducated industrial workers of Britain. The Morlocks still maintain the old machines, though they have lost all memory of their functions. Wells' descriptions of these creatures, who dwell underground, afraid of the light of day, were clearly influenced by his childhood experiences in cellars. Readers recognized and sympathized with this symbolic reference to the bleak lives of many Victorian servants and workers.

These nineteenth-century factory workers toiled long, hard hours for little pay to produce fancy hats bought by the wealthy aristocracy. Wells' The Time Machine *described a future civilization evolved from these two interdependent classes of people.*

In the story, the Eloi are the descendants of the rich, upper-class people of Britain. Here, Wells was commenting on an idea, believed by many critics of the British class system, that members of the upper classes could not maintain their luxurious life-styles without the toil of the lower-class workers, farmers, and servants. The formerly upper-class Eloi have become totally dependent upon the Morlocks, and have even become food for these descendants of the lower classes. Many readers found this idea of the servants becoming the masters both riveting and frightening.

The Time Machine appealed to many readers for another reason: The book did not have a happy ending. Most Victorian writers who described the future painted rosy pictures of humanity evolving to higher levels and civilization advancing. Many people found this idea comforting, but others, like Wells, wondered if it was realistic. Instead, he showed a hopeless, desolate future, one in which humans have

The downtrodden working class found a sympathetic voice in H.G. Wells. Wells wanted his writings to make people think and to inspire them to make the world a better place.

degenerated rather than advanced. His was a vision of evolution working in reverse.

Yet, in this tale of doom and despair, Wells provided a glimmer of hope. At the book's conclusion, after the Time Traveler has disappeared in his machine, his friend comments:

> One cannot choose but wonder. Will he ever return? . . . He, I know . . . thought but cheerlessly of the Advancement of Mankind, and saw in the growing pile of civilization only a foolish heaping [of war, misery, and pollution] that must inevitably fall back upon and destroy its makers in the end. If that is so, it remains for us to live as though it were not so.[21]

By saying that people should "live as though it were not so," Wells was stating a major belief that was part of his own outlook on life. He was suggesting that no matter what problems occur in the future, people should never give up. They should constantly strive to build a better

---

To Live as Though It Were Not So

In the finale of The Time Machine, *Wells comments both negatively and positively about human nature. On the one hand, he says that civilization is a foolish waste that will eventually topple. On the other, he draws attention to the goodness of the human spirit. After the Time Traveler disappears forever, his friend ponders some flowers given to the Traveler by a young woman of the far future.*

"One cannot choose but wonder. Will he ever return? It may be that he swept back into the past, and fell among the blood-drinking, hairy savages of the Age of Unpolished Stone; into the abysses [deep pits] of the Cretacious Sea; or among the grotesque saurians [dinosaurs] . . . of Jurassic times. . . . Or did he go forward, into one of the nearer ages, in which men are still men, but with the riddles of our own time answered and its wearisome problems solved? . . . He, I know—for the question had been discussed among us long before the Time Machine was made—thought but cheerlessly of the Advancement of Mankind, and saw in the growing pile of civilization only a foolish heaping that must inevitably fall back upon and destroy its makers in the end. If that is so, it remains for us to live as though it were not so. But to me the future is still black and blank—is a vast ignorance, lit at a few casual places by the memory of his story. And I have by me, for my comfort, two strange white flowers—shrivelled now, and brown and flat and brittle—to witness that even when mind and strength had gone, gratitude and a mutual tenderness still lived on in the heart of man."

world. The desire to change the world would soon become one of the main goals of Wells' life. As Lovat Dickson put it, "The determination to live as though it were not so was to animate Wells' whole career as a writer."[22]

The success of *The Time Machine* not only established Wells as a famous writer, but it also brought him significant financial rewards. More publishers wanted his work and were willing to pay larger sums to get it. As a teacher, he had earned less than two hundred British pounds a year.

In 1895, the year *The Time Machine* appeared, he made nearly eight hundred pounds. Excited over this success, he and Jane were married on October 27, 1895. They now looked forward to a prosperous life, and Wells wrote to several friends saying he expected his success to continue. He had good reason to feel optimistic. He could write well and quickly, and there was a ready market for his work. As Wells' thirtieth birthday approached, he was on his way to becoming a well-to-do and admired man of letters.

3 The Scientific Romances

H.G. Wells' success with *The Time Machine* enabled him and Jane to move away from the noise and dirt of the city. He was sure that the quiet atmosphere in the country would allow him to work better. In September 1895, they rented a house in Woking, a picturesque village about twelve miles west of London. The comfortable home with its own garden was within walking distance of the main rail line. This made it easy for Wells to travel into the city on business when he needed to. Once they had moved in, he happily found that the move to the country did help him concentrate. He began turning out short stories, articles, novels, and outlines for future novels at a feverish pace. In the first two years alone he wrote five novels and more than one hundred shorter works. "It was an astonishing burst of activity," commented Norman Mackenzie, "for an inexperienced writer with indifferent [sometimes poor] health. . . . [Wells averaged] one book and thirty stories or articles every six months, and well over a million words in all."[23]

Among the writings Wells turned out in the period from 1895 to 1901 were some of his best and most famous works. Woking and its surrounding countryside became the settings for two novels. One was *The War of the Worlds,* the story of the invasion of Earth by beings from the planet Mars. The other was *The Invisible Man,* about a mad scientist who becomes invisible and terrorizes society. Like *The Time Machine,* these novels explored the

Wells and Jane pose in their garden in Woking, twelve miles from London. Freed from the noise and distractions of the city, Wells turned out books and stories as never before.

mysteries of nature and the fantastic possibilities of science. Also like his first novel, they served as warnings about the unfair and undesirable customs and policies of Wells' own society. During this first major writing period of his career, Wells wrote or conceived of four other novels expressing these themes. They were *The Island of Dr. Moreau, The First Men in the Moon, The Food of the Gods,* and *In the Days of the Comet.*

These seven novels were markedly different from most of the literature of Wells' day. Most books and stories of the late 1890s dealt with real-life characters and situations. By contrast, Wells' seven novels dealt with incredible machines and

An illustration depicts a scene described in Wells' novel The First Men in the Moon. *Wells created a new category of literature—the scientific romance, which was the forerunner of science fiction.*

A cover illustration for a reprint of one of Wells' stories about scientific experiments gone awry. A real-life shipwreck gave Wells a starting point for this imaginative fantasy.

weapons, alien beings, mad scientists, and catastrophes of nature. All of them explored the process of evolution and the bizarre paths it might take. At that time, the field of science fiction did not yet exist, and no one knew what to call Wells' strange new tales. The books all dealt with science, but they were also highly romantic, in the sense that they were filled with adventure and mystery. So Wells and his editors coined the term *scientific romances* to describe the seven novels.

Creating Atmosphere

For the first of the scientific romances he wrote in Woking, *The War of the Worlds,* Wells carefully scouted out villages, roads, rivers, and other actual settings in England.

Attack of the Giant Rats

Wells' ability to create a mood of suspense and horror is illustrated by this excerpt from The Food of the Gods. *A man driving a horse-drawn buggy is suddenly attacked by gigantic rats.*

"And then he saw quite distinctly . . . the curved back of—some big animal, he couldn't tell what, going along in quick convulsive leaps. . . . He cracked his whip . . . and then in a flash the rats were at him! He had passed a gate and as he did so, the foremost rat came leaping over into the road. The thing sprang upon him out of vagueness [dim lighting] into the utmost clearness, the sharp, eager, round-eared face . . . the pink webbed forefeet of the beast. . . . He did not recognize it as a rat because of its size. . . . The doctor . . . slashed [with his whip] with all his strength . . . and he slashed again and again, heedless and unaware of the second pursuer that gained upon his offside. . . . No one knows how the horse came down, whether it stumbled or whether the rat on the offside really got home with one of those slashing downstrokes of the incisors [teeth]. . . . The horse reared up with the rat biting again at its throat, and fell sideways. . . . As the buggy came down, the . . . lamp smashed, and suddenly poured a flare of blazing oil, a thud of white flame into the struggle. . . . The doctor yelled and hammered. . . . 'I don't know what they *are!*' he repeated several times . . . [and escaped into a nearby house]. . . . And when the fire was out the giant rats came back, took the dead horse, dragged it across the churchyard into the brickfield and ate at it until it was dawn, none even then daring to disturb them."

Wells' scientific romances later proved to be good material for science fiction movies. A giant rat attacks a man in this scene from the movie version of The Food of the Gods.

The tranquil English countryside around Wells' home in Woking served as a setting for several of the writer's stories.

In great detail, he planned the landing spots and travels of the attacking Martians. These alien creatures landed their spacecraft in rural areas like Woking, then marched on paths of destruction into the hearts of cities like London.

In addition to Woking, Wells chose other areas he knew well as settings, including South Kensington, the site of London University. Later, a letter to a friend described the places he chose to destroy. "I completely wreck and sack Woking," he explained, "killing my neighbors in painful and eccentric [odd] ways—then proceed . . . to London, which I sack, selecting South Kensington for feats of peculiar atrocity [cruelty]."[24] Wells' selection of real places as backdrops for his stories was significant. By describing in detail places the readers were familiar with, he made the bizarre events of his plots more believable. The following example of the realistic atmosphere he created using this method is from *The War of the Worlds*. The narrator and some

other people flee from the Martians through real locations in the English countryside:

Away across the road the woods beyond Ham and Pertersham were still afire. Twickenham [a village] was uninjured by either heat ray or Black Smoke, and there were more people about here, though none could give us news. . . . I have an impression that many of the houses here were still occupied by scared inhabitants, too frightened even for flight. . . . I remember most vividly three smashed bicycles in a heap, pounded into the road by the wheels of subsequent carts. We crossed Richmond Bridge about half past eight. . . . Here again on the Surrey side were dead bodies—a heap near the approach to the station; but we had no glimpse of the Martians until we were some ways towards Barnes. . . . Up the hill Richmond town was burning briskly.[25]

From Across the Gulf of Space

The War of the Worlds had been inspired by Wells' earlier fascination with astronomy. Mars had made an unusually close approach to earth in 1877 when Wells was eleven. At that time, the well-known Italian astronomer Giovanni Schiaparelli claimed he saw *canali,* or waterways, on the planet. That word translated into English as "canals," which implied purposely constructed waterways. The American astronomer Percival Lowell also said he saw canals on Mars in the 1890s. Thus, in the

American astronomer Percival Lowell claimed to see canals on the surface of Mars. The possibility of life on Mars inspired one of Wells' most famous novels.

An invading Martian spaceship lands on the edge of a dark English wood in this illustration from Wells' The War of the Worlds.

late 1800s there was a great deal of popular interest in the possibility of intelligent life on Mars.

Wells gave considerable thought to what such Martian life might be like. In *The War of the Worlds,* he imagined the Martians as a dying race on a desert planet. In his scenario, the building of canals was a last desperate attempt to conserve water to grow food. The need for water provided the Martians with a motive for invading the lush, green earth. In "The Man of the Year Million" Wells had envisioned humans evolving into creatures with enlarged heads to encase their expanded brains. The Martians in his novel have evolved even further. They are essentially huge heads with tentacles that they use to crawl around and manipulate objects.

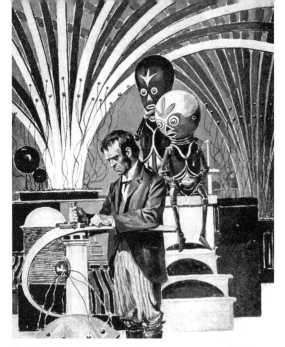

In his tales of invaders from outer space, Wells imagined highly evolved aliens as little more than huge brains with hands and feet.

Wells purposely used the images of these alien creatures to create a feeling of horror, as in the narrator's first encounter with a Martian:

> Two large dark-coloured eyes were regarding me steadfastly [with great interest]. The mass that framed them, the head of the thing, it was rounded, and had, one might say, a face. There was a mouth under the eyes, the lipless brim of which quivered and panted, and dropped saliva. The whole creature heaved and pulsated convulsively [in spasms]. A . . . [thin tentacle] gripped the edge of the cylinder, another swayed in the air. Those who have never seen a living Martian can scarcely imagine the strange horror of its appearance. . . . There was something fungoid in the oily brown skin, something in the clumsy . . . movements [of the creature]

unspeakably nasty. Even at this first encounter, this first glimpse, I was overcome with disgust and dread.[26]

Wells' Martians are more than just physically repulsive. He suggested that they have evolved beyond the capacity for emotions like love and pity. He portrayed them as cold, calculating, and unfeeling. Nowhere in literature is such cold alien intelligence described more chillingly than in the ominous opening of *The War of the Worlds*:

> No one would have believed in the last years of the nineteenth century that this world was being watched keenly and closely by intelligences greater than man's and yet as mortal as his own; that as men busied themselves about their various concerns they were scrutinised [observed] and studied, perhaps almost as narrowly as a man with a microscope might scrutinise the transient

In this illustration from The War of the Worlds, *Martian machines of destruction use death rays to ravage the English countryside.*

[short-lived] creatures that swarm and multiply in a drop of water. . . . Across the gulf of space, minds that are to our minds as ours are to those of the beasts . . . intellects vast and cool and unsympathetic, regarded this earth with envious eyes, and slowly and surely drew their plans against us.[27]

In the novel, these "vast intellects" use devastating heat rays and other weapons to subdue humanity. In the end, their inability to cope with earthly germs stops the invaders.

Touching a Public Nerve

When *The War of the Worlds* was published in 1898, readers and critics reacted with enthusiasm. They saw the story of the Martian invasion, like *The Time Machine,* as a colorful tale of strange beings and exciting adventure. The book also seemed to touch a special nerve with the reading public—the fascination with the idea of life on Mars. In addition, many critics praised Wells for the way he used the story to speak out against the abuses of British imperialism. An imperialist nation is one that extends its influence over foreign peoples by military or other forceful means. By the end of the nineteenth century, many people in Britain had begun to criticize the British policy of expanding and maintaining a worldwide empire. As a model for the novel, Wells singled out the violent methods used by British settlers in Tasmania, an island south of Australia. In the "black war," of the early 1800s, the British had used guns and other superior weapons to wipe out the helpless native blacks. Wells compared the treatment of human beings by the Martians to the slaughter of the Tasmanians by British settlers.

Wells criticized the policy of imperialism in a different way in another of his scientific romances—*The First Men in the Moon.* Here, a group of humans travel to the moon and meddle in the affairs of intelligent creatures called Selenites. Instead of aliens invading the earth, Wells shows earth people causing the downfall of another race. Readers were moved by the sadness of this concept and by Wells' riveting descriptions of lunar landscapes. The novel sold many copies, earning Wells more than two thousand pounds in the first two years after its release. Practically everything else he wrote during these years sold just as well.

The huge financial success of the works Wells completed at Woking between 1895 and 1898 made him a wealthy man.

The cover of a popular 1920s fantasy magazine depicts a scene from The Invisible Man, *Wells' story which warns of the dangers of uncontrolled science.*

Invisibility Aids in Murder

The Invisible Man *was one of Wells' most vivid warnings about how dangerous science could be in the wrong hands. In the book, the scientist Griffin, who has become insane after turning himself invisible, explains to his associate Kemp the powers that go with invisibility.*

"We have to consider all that invisibility means, all that it does not mean. It means little advantage for eavesdropping and so forth—one makes sounds. It's of little help, a little help perhaps—in housebreaking and so forth. Once you've caught me you could easily imprison me. But on the other hand I am hard to catch. This invisibility, in fact, is only good in two cases: It's useful in getting away, it's useful in approaching. It's particularly useful, therefore, in killing. I can walk round a man, whatever weapon he has, choose any point, strike as I like. Dodge as I like. Escape as I like.

Kemp's hand went to his moustache. Was that a movement downstairs?

'And it is killing we must do, Kemp.'

'It is killing we must do,' repeated Kemp. 'I'm listening to your plan, Griffin, but I'm not agreeing, mind. *Why* killing?'

'Not wanton killing, but a judicious [clever] slaying. The point is, they know there is an Invisible Man—as well as we know there is an Invisible Man. And that Invisible Man, Kemp, must now establish a Reign of Terror. Yes—no doubt it's startling. But I mean it. A Reign of Terror. He must take some town like your Burdock and terrify and dominate it. He must issue his orders. He can do that in a thousand ways—scraps of paper thrust under doors would suffice. And all who disobey his orders he must kill, and kill all who would defend them.'"

Because of his generous nature, he was quick to share his newfound success. He sent money to Isabel, whose welfare he was still concerned about. He also began giving money to his parents, who remained separated. He still visited them as often as possible and openly spoke about the debt he felt he owed them. Expressing this gratitude in a letter to them, he wrote, "Whatever success I have, you are responsible for the beginnings of it. However hard up you were when I was a youngster you let me have paper and pencils, books . . . and so forth and if I haven't my mother to thank for my imagination and my father for skill, where did I get these qualities?"[28] The extra money also gave Wells and Jane reason to start talking about having a house built, one they would design themselves.

A Realist of the Fantastic

But the plans for a new home had to be temporarily postponed because Wells had several more bouts of kidney trouble. Often bedridden, he continued to write dozens of pages a week. While still in Woking, he wrote another scientific romance—*The Invisible Man*. It was the story of Dr. Griffin, a scientist who discovers a strange chemical formula. When he drinks it, he becomes invisible to the human eye. Unfortunately, the chemical alters his mind, changing him into a dangerous maniac. He terrifies villages and murders several people before being hunted down and killed.

As in his other romances, Wells tried to show how science can become dangerous. Scientists themselves might be corrupted by their discoveries and harm society instead of helping it. In *The War of the Worlds*, the Martians' heat rays are instruments of power wielded by creatures without emotion or pity. Similarly, Griffin's cloak of invisibility gives him power over others, a power he uses to maim and kill. "It is the killing we must do . . . ," the insane Griffin tells another scientist in the novel. "That Invisible Man . . . must establish a Reign of Terror. . . . He must take some town, and terrify and dominate it."[29] The ravings of Wells' mad scientist explore how important it is for scientists to maintain control of their discoveries. Both *The Invisible Man*

Touches of Humor

Wells was capable of great humor, as is seen in this excerpt from his June 27, 1904 letter to his publisher, Frederick Macmillan. The subject was what to title his scientific romance about the discovery of a miracle nutrient that produces giantism.

"*The Food of the Gods on Earth* is so detestable [bad] a title it keeps me awake at nights. . . . What do you say to *Heraklephorbia: The Food of the Gods,* making the former title a sort of second title? That 'On Earth' is intolerably weak. 'Heraklephorbia' is no doubt a hard-looking word, but it's not too difficult to pronounce. It arrests attention. The French title is to be '*Place Aux Geants,*' the Italian '*Ecco i Giganti,*' neither of which gives any tolerable English equivalent. The plain fact is that *The Food of the Gods* is *the* title and I can't stand the idea of any other. Suppose we were to give the book a long title: *The Food of the Gods and How It Came to Earth* and trust people to drop the last six words. I really do think that is quite the best thing to do—far better than adding 'on earth.' Why 'on earth'? You will be wishing it anywhere else very soon."

Wells' Quickness Leads to Chastising

Wells' ability to write so well and so quickly amazed his friends and associates. In 1895, his editor, W.E. Henley, praised his newest book, The Wonderful Visit, *and cautioned Wells not to work so fast as to sacrifice quality.*

"There is brains in the book; brains to any extent. Brains; & character & humour . . . for heaven's sake, take care of yourself. You have a unique talent; and—you have produced three books, at least, within the year, & are up to the elbows in a fourth! It is magnificent, of course; but it can't be literature. . . . I believe in your imagination; & I don't want to see it foundered [wrecked]. I believe in your future; & I don't want to see it commonplaced. And you really frighten me: you work so easily . . . but you could also do better—far better; & to begin with, you must begin by taking yourself more seriously."

and *The War of the Worlds,* Wells later said, should stand as warnings. They should remind people that uncontrolled power and the use of intelligence without sympathy can be dangerous.

The public response to *The Invisible Man* was overwhelmingly favorable. As usual, Wells' ability to tell a fantastic tale in a realistic manner was the key to his popularity. After reading the novel, the writer Joseph Conrad singled out this special talent in a letter of praise to Wells. Wrote Conrad, "I am always powerfully impressed by your work. Impressed is *the* word, O Realist of the Fantastic!"[30]

Wells received hundreds of such fan letters. Most of them came from people who were intrigued with the way he showed science unlocking the mysteries of nature. Many letter writers said they had developed an interest in science after reading his books. There is no evidence that scientists themselves heeded, or even

heard, the warnings of *The Invisible Man* and the other scientific romances. But the reading public found the books entertaining and thought-provoking. *The Food of the Gods* and *The Island of Dr. Moreau,* both tales of scientists tampering with human evolution, added to Wells' fame and fortune. So did *In the Days of the Comet,* a story of science building a better world after a giant comet's passing alters civilization.

Into the Treasure House

By 1899, Wells' health was much better, and he and Jane decided to go ahead with their plans to build a house. They moved to a temporary residence in Sandgate, a quiet seaside town about fifty miles southeast of London. There, they oversaw the building of Spade House, on which

In 1900, Wells supervised the building of Spade House, his and Jane's dream home, in the seaside town of Sandgate.

Befitting the visionary Wells, the interior of Spade House was extremely modern and included electric lights.

construction was begun in February 1900. By December 8, the work was completed and they moved into what a friend called their "treasure house on the seashore."

Wells and Jane greatly enjoyed the privacy and comfort of Spade House, and

The Wells' two sons, George, nicknamed Gip (right), and Frank, were born in Spade House in 1901 and 1903, respectively.

soon decided they were ready to raise a family. In the summer of 1901, Wells wrote to his friend, novelist Arnold Bennett, "Mrs. Wells and I have been collaborating [working together] . . . in the invention of a human being."[31] On July 17, Jane had a boy whom they named George Philip. Because everyone called Wells H.G., they nicknamed the boy G.P., which soon became Gip. Two years later, Wells and Jane "invented" a second son, Frank.

For Wells, the move to Spade House and the birth of his sons were parts of a larger change in his life and attitudes. A new century was also beginning, one that he hoped might bring peace and happiness for humanity. For several years, his writings had expressed his doubts and worries about science and progress. But the idea that humanity might decline had represented only one side of his thinking. Now, he felt the urge to explore the other side—the idea that human beings might progress and improve their situation. Feeling very optimistic, he began to visualize the marvels that science might bring. Boldly, he took on the role of prophet for humanity's future.

4 A Gift of Prophecy

Wells' move to Spade House in Sandgate signaled the beginning of a new phase in his life and his writing career. It was the beginning of the twentieth century. As they have at the beginning of every new century, people looked forward to a fresh start. They hoped that society would be able to eliminate many of the problems of the past and build a better future. Wells was infected by this optimism like everyone else. And there were many other new elements in his life. There were his children, Gip and Frank, for whom he installed an elaborate toy train layout in the spacious nursery. There were also many new friends. Because of his success, Wells met dozens of well-known literary figures,

including the novelist Henry James and the playwright George Bernard Shaw. The Wellses held many parties in Spade House for their growing group of acquaintances. In addition, new publishers offered him projects, opening the door to new possibilities for expressing his ideas.

Envisioning a More Positive Future

Part of Wells' new attitude was a feeling of optimism about humanity's future. The images of the future he had described in the scientific romances had been mostly

Frank and Gip Wells enjoy their toy train set at Spade House. A new home and family gave Wells a positive outlook on the future. His work began to reflect this new optimism.

Wells' utopia would have had no poor people and no unwanted pregnancies. He wanted his readers to take action to reform society.

negative. They had been bleak scenarios depicting human decline, doom, or extinction. Shortly after moving to Spade House, Wells gave a lecture at the Royal Institution in London that illustrated just how much his thinking had changed. Referring to the hopeless futures pictured in his earlier works, he said:

> One must admit that it is impossible to show why certain things should not utterly destroy and end the entire human race and story; why night should not presently come down and make all our dreams and efforts vain. . . . That of all such nightmares is the most consistently convincing. . . . And yet one doesn't believe it. At least I do not. And I do not believe in those things because I have come to believe in certain other things, in the coherency [order] and purpose in the world and in the greatness of human destiny. Worlds may freeze and suns may perish, but I believe there stirs something within us now that can never die again.[32]

Along with Wells' new optimism about the future came a different view of the part he and his writings should play in shaping that future. Before, he had been merely a social commentator. Through his writings, he had delivered warnings about social ills to his readers while entertaining them. Now, he began to feel that he could and should do more. He should direct more of his energies as a writer and as a person to changing society for the better. This fundamental shift in attitude was significant for Wells, casting him in the role of social crusader. "Like that figure of Atlas which stood in my father's shop window," he later recalled, "I sustained the whole world upon my shoulders."[33] He would maintain this strong, self-imposed sense of responsibility for helping the human race for the rest of his life.

Beginning in 1901, Wells chose a new writing form to express his positive views about humanity's future. He hoped this form would instruct his readers as well as entertain them. Using both fiction and nonfiction, he began to prophesy, or predict, various inventions, customs, social systems and governments of the future. He usually envisioned utopias, ideal societies or worlds, in which war, poverty, crime, and other problems have been eliminated. Wells believed that these writings would become examples, or models, inspiring and motivating people to change society for the better. He expressed this belief in a letter to Arnold Bennett:

> I believe quite simply that a first-class boom and uproar and discussion about . . . [my utopian writings] will do an infinite amount of good in the country and to you at least there is no need to put my belief in breeches [be modest]. I think I am safe to get most of the comfortable *educated* London public but I dream of getting it read by parsons and country doctors and all that sort and going much wider than my publishers dream. I think there are a multitude of interesting . . . [ideas about the future to explore] . . . home conveniences, the status of unmarried girls, cooking . . . building, dress, etc. that ought to be *groundbait* [attractive ideas] for the big public.[34]

By predicting and describing new inventions and customs, Wells hoped to show

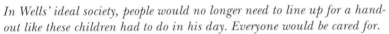

In Wells' ideal society, people would no longer need to line up for a hand-out like these children had to do in his day. Everyone would be cared for.

An Unattractive Personality

Wells' friend Beatrice Webb never liked or appreciated Wells and Jane as much as she pretended to when socializing with them. Webb often coldly analyzed people, as evidenced by the following February 28, 1902 entry excerpted from her diary. At this time, Wells was beginning to predict the changes of the future in his first utopian books.

"Wells is an interesting though somewhat unattractive personality except for his agreeable disposition and intellectual vivacity [energy]. . . . He is a good instrument for popularizing ideas, and he gives as many ideas as he receives. . . . Altogether it is refreshing to talk to a man who has shaken himself loose from so many of the current assumptions [accepted beliefs] and is looking at life as an explorer of a new world. His wife is a pretty little person with a strong will, mediocre [average] intelligence and somewhat small nature. She has carefully molded herself in dress, manners and even accent to take her place in any society her husband's talents may lead them into. But it is all rather artificial, from the sweetness of her smile to her interest in public affairs. However, she provides him with a charming well-ordered home, though I should imagine her constant companionship was somewhat stifling. They are both of them well-bred in their pleasant tempers, careful consideration of the feelings of others, quick apprehension [understanding] of new conventions and requirements, but they both of them lack ease and repose [calmness], and she has an ugly absence of spontaneity [originality] of thought and feeling."

his readers that the future could be both exciting and more comfortable. They would then, he hoped, be moved to help bring about the social and political reforms he advocated. The desire to bring about beneficial changes in society was the purpose behind the many utopian works that Wells produced, off and on, for the rest of his life.

In the Hands of "Capable Men"

Wells' future utopias were almost always socialist societies. Socialism is a political system in which the government owns and administers the land, factories, and other institutions. In an ideal socialist state, there can be no poverty or inequality. The government looks after all citizens, ensuring that they receive equal treatment and opportunity. Wells had been exposed to socialist ideas in his college days. Over the years, he had become convinced that adopting some form of socialism would be the best way for people to reform society.

In his utopian writings, Wells nearly always envisioned a handful of honest, caring individuals, much like himself, running the socialist state. He called them "reasonable" and "a new mass of capable men." They would be, he predicted, mostly scientists with a strong sense of duty to their fellow human beings. These enlightened leaders would eliminate poverty, crime, and the unfair class system. The laboring masses of industrial workers would receive better pay, housing, and education. And those with wealth and power would use their money and position to aid the unfortunate. In addition, Britain and other powerful countries would end their domination of foreign peoples. The time,

energy, and money needed to maintain empires would be spent improving conditions at home. All of these reforms, Wells believed, could be achieved through the application of a socialist system. And his positive futuristic writings would help people build such a system.

Unfortunately for Wells, this vision had a major drawback, one that would affect his later happiness and outlook on life. He expected the sweeping social changes he advocated to happen in the span of only a few years. This goal was totally unrealistic. Despite his great intellect, Wells did not grasp just how difficult a task reshaping the world would be. His view of his own role in this enormous task was also distorted. He seriously overestimated the impact a single popular writer could have in bringing about social change. Although his earlier works had made people think, as he had intended, readers still looked at them mainly as entertainment. Most people continued to view his writings in this way throughout his career.

The social reforms that could save a family from living in dirty, crowded slums like this did not happen fast enough for Wells. He was disappointed when his writings did not change the world immediately.

Wells predicted that humans would fly before the year 1950. The Wright brothers' historic airplane flight in 1903 fulfilled Wells' prophecy nearly fifty years sooner. Wells' date was closer than most. The New York Times, for example, had stated that humans would not conquer flight for millions of years.

The casual attitude of Wells' readers toward his early utopian writings frustrated him. Extremely idealistic, he sincerely expected people to take his ideas about social reform seriously and then act upon them. It perplexed him that "reasonable" people in positions of influence and power did not quickly use his ideas as blueprints to restructure society. Wells failed to see why intelligent, rational people did not immediately accept his views about reforming society. He would remain frustrated about the attitudes of his readers for the rest of his life, stubbornly refusing to accept the idea that major social change would take many generations.

Anticipations of a New Society

The first of Wells' books that were designed to point society toward a better future was *Anticipations of the Reaction of* *Mechanical and Scientific Progress upon Human Life and Thought*. Published in December 1901, it was the forerunner of all his later writings prophesying a utopian future. *Anticipations* was a collection of nonfiction articles in which Wells envisioned scientists, his "capable men," eventually taking control of society. The new leaders, he proposed, would establish "a world state with a common language and a common rule." It would be a "new world order," said Wells, "the New Republic. All over the world its roads, its standards, its laws and its apparatus [methods] of control will run [things]."[35] There would be, Wells predicted, automobiles and airplanes to make traveling faster. There would also be countless work-saving devices to make life at home and in the workplace easier.

The new order Wells envisioned did not include "unfit" individuals such as criminals. Nor did it include masses of unwanted children growing up in poverty and ignorance, or the hopelessly poor people created by the Industrial Revolution. He suggested that science would provide the means to eliminate these unfit and unwanted people. Researchers would find new and better forms of birth control to eliminate unwanted pregnancies. Some people, he predicted, would opt for sterilization, or surgery that eliminates the ability to reproduce. With no unwanted children, society could afford to support and educate everyone. The result, said Wells, would be a poverty-free, crime-free society in which each person served a useful function.

Anticipations was a great success. It sold even more copies than Wells' earlier novels, which was a great surprise to his publisher, the Macmillan Company. Normally, nonfiction, especially nonfiction of such a serious nature, did not sell nearly as well as fiction. To Wells' delight, Macmillan quickly ran out of copies and had to print more.

Wells' continued success and fame brought many social invitations from well-known and wealthy people. He and Jane often spent weekends in elegant country homes throughout southern England. In return, they invited their new friends to stay at Spade House. Their friend Henry James summed up the admiration that members of the upper classes had for Wells at this time. "You'd say that he had everything," remarked James. He had his loving wife and children, "his . . . gift [talent], his . . . popularity . . . his stately treasure house on the sea shore, richly endowed with the splendid gift of youth . . ."[36] In addition, Wells had accomplished something his parents had never thought possible. By talent and force of will, he had risen from the dismal life of the lower classes to the comfortable world of the well-to-do.

A Prophet of Gadgets

But along with the benefits of his success, Wells also experienced profound disappointment. He wanted his writing to stimulate social change. But he soon realized that most of his readers were not particularly inspired by the social reforms he had described. Instead, they were fascinated by the individual scientific and technical marvels he predicted, especially such devices as automobiles and airplanes. Though it was not his intention, *Anticipations* established Wells as a prophet of future inventions and gadgets. Once again, it was his ability as an entertainer, rather than as a reformer, that the public admired. In fact, many readers did not believe that such marvelous inventions would ever actually exist. They saw them as elements of a diverting and enjoyable kind of fantasy. This frustrated Wells, who wanted people to take the book more seriously. He continued to turn out similar prophetic literature, hoping his ideas would inspire social change.

In the following few years, readers and critics continued to respond favorably to most of Wells' utopian books. *A Modern Utopia, Mankind in the Making,* and *The World Set Free* all outlined the same kind of ideal future society he had envisioned in *Anticipations.* But none of these works brought about the social reforms Wells was working for. Each owed its popularity to the author's colorful and exciting predictions about new inventions and how they would affect people's lives.

Wells' uncanny ability to foresee the use of technology is shown by the fact that so many of his predictions have become reality. For example, he foretold that scientists would unlock vast powers hidden inside the atom. These powers, he said, would be used both in weapons of destruction and to produce energy. He brilliantly predicted the strategic value of tanks in land warfare and also insisted that humans would build and fly airplanes. In 1901, two years before the Wright brothers' historic flight, the *New York Times* predicted that it would take up to ten million years for people to conquer the air. In that same year, in *Anticipations,* Wells wrote that "very probably before 1950, a successful aeroplane will have soared and come home safe and sound."[37] Though he did not pinpoint the precise year, his time frame was far more accurate than anyone else's.

In addition to the inventions themselves, Wells often foresaw the impact they would have on society. For instance, he did more than just predict the advent of automobiles. He also described in detail the things autos would bring about—networks of highways, the growth of suburbs, and traffic jams.

Occasionally he was wrong in predicting the importance of an invention. A prominent example was his failure to see the value of the submarine for warfare and deep-sea exploration. "I must confess," he wrote, "that my imagination . . . refuses to see any sort of submarine do anything but suffocate its crew and founder at sea."[38]

A Novel About Himself

Wells' writings predicting the future were not his only attempt to bring about social change. In 1905, he decided to put on paper an idea he had been mulling over for several years. It was a realistic novel titled *Kipps: The Story of a Simple Soul,* which

was to be based on his own childhood and adolescent experiences. *Kipps* was the story of the struggles of Artie Kipps, a boy of the working classes. Drawing upon memories of his past, Wells filled the book with realistic and touching details that made young Kipps' character come alive. "Of all . . . [Wells'] books," remarked Lovat Dickson, "*Kipps* meant the most to him. It was the first long novel of character he had embarked on, and it was about himself and the things he knew of. . . . H.G.'s experiences in the drapery . . . are faithfully reflected in Kipps' . . . adventures in the same field."[39]

Wells' strong pride in *Kipps* and affection for it are evident in a letter he sent to his publisher describing the novel:

> *Kipps* is essentially a novel, built on modern lines, about the development of a single character. . . . *Kipps* is designed to present a typical member of the English lower middle-class in all its pitiful limitation and feebleness, and . . . provides a sustained and fairly exhaustive criticism of the ideals and ways of life of the great mass of middle-class English people. The . . . characters . . . are all based on the most careful and exhaustive study of living types: you must judge for yourself how far they are alive. . . . There has been the most strenuous effort [on my part] to avoid pushing the jokes home or any vulgar insistence upon the emotion of the situations. I have sought before all things the glow of reality. It's an infernally good book as a matter of fact . . . and I refuse absolutely to be modest about it.[40]

By showing the sad conditions people of the lower classes endured, Wells hoped

Decades before H.G. Wells, Charles Dickens (left) wrote about the dehumanizing influences of the Industrial Revolution in England.

Mr. Squeers, an abusive schoolmaster in Dickens' novel Nicholas Nickleby. *Dickens' story spotlighted teachers' abuse of pupils and ignited public outrage that led to school reforms.*

to arouse the conscience of the reading public. Most of his readers were of the middle and upper classes, which included lawmakers. He reasoned that the novel might move these political leaders to push for social reforms. This was, to some degree, what Charles Dickens had accomplished with some of his novels several decades earlier. For instance, Dickens' vivid descriptions of British schoolmasters beating their students in *Nicholas Nickleby* inspired public outrage. This pressured the government into investigating and closing down many schools. Wells hoped that *Kipps* might similarly pressure lawmakers into starting socialist welfare programs to aid the poor.

Macmillan published the novel late in 1905, and within a year it had sold more than twelve thousand copies, Wells' biggest single sale to date. *Kipps* did not inspire social change as Wells had hoped, but it touched people's hearts. Reviews were glowing, most echoing the opinion of Henry James, who wrote to Wells, "[The book] left me prostrate [flattened] with admiration. . . . I am lost in amazement at the diversity of your genius . . . what am I to say about Kipps, but that. . . . He is not so much a masterpiece as a . . . gem . . . of such brilliancy of *true* truth."[41]

A Storm in a Teacup

While writing *Kipps* and his early utopian books, Wells concluded that his literary efforts were not enough of a commitment to bettering society. He felt he should do more and decided to get involved in politics. In February 1903, he joined the Fabian Society, a socialist group whose official aim was to restructure society, making all institutions as fair and ethical as possible. Some Fabian goals were to abolish the class system and poverty, to give all citizens equal opportunities in life, and to build a more democratic society. The Fabians believed that these goals should be

Playwright George Bernard Shaw sponsored Wells' membership in the Fabian Society, a political reform group.

achieved by gradual reforms rather than by violent revolution. Since all of the group's members were well-to-do and influential, they attempted to pressure lawmakers and

Writer Sidney Webb and his wife Beatrice were part of Wells' social circle. Like Wells, the Webbs were members of the Fabian Society.

"You Are Not Amiable Enough"

Wells' energetic and forceful attempts to remold the Fabian Society were not appreciated by some of the group's older members. They felt his lectures to them sometimes insulted their intelligence and that he pushed for radical changes without the consent of all the members. Wells' friend George Bernard Shaw, who had sponsored Wells' entry into the group, scolded him in a letter dated March 24, 1906.

"You may say you are making superhuman efforts to be amiable [friendly]. No doubt you are; but you are not amiable enough, in spite of your efforts. And you are too reckless of etiquette [bad-mannered]. . . . You had no more right to report that debate than you had to write our checks; and that is just one of the things that the human animal will not stand. . . . Even if your report had been approximately accurate instead of a blaze of wanton mendacity [falsehoods] from beginning to end . . . *any* human committee—would have . . . [objected to being dictated to]. You must study people's corns when you go clog dancing. Generally speaking, you must . . . not play the critical outsider and the satirist. We are all very clever; and long ago we have come to understand that we must not play our cleverness off against one another for the mere fun of it. . . . There are limits to our powers of enduring humiliations that are totally undeserved. . . . You haven't discovered the real difficulties of democratic work; and you assume that your own folly and ill will accounts for their results. Give my love to Jane, that well behaved woman. Why she married you (I being single at the time) the Life Force [God] only knows."

George Bernard Shaw, Wells' candid friend and advisor.

public officials. Many Fabians were writers, the best-known being George Bernard Shaw and Sidney Webb. They often used their written works to preach about socialism and to educate the public about their ideas.

Despite these efforts, there were only about seven hundred Fabians in 1903 and few aggressively promoted the group's aims. This frustrated Wells from the day that Shaw sponsored him as a new member. The forceful and energetic Wells wanted the group to expand its membership and be more aggressive in pushing its ideas. The Fabians, he said, "ought to have 7,000 members instead of 700 and everything else to scale."[42]

Wells made several attempts to assume leadership of the Fabians. He did this by promoting himself in speeches to the group and running in the society's elections. But in each vote he met with opposition from the older members. They believed that social change should happen slowly and felt that Wells wanted to move too fast. He was too idealistic and reckless, they said. Eventually, Wells concluded that he was wasting his time with the Fabians, and he quit the organization in 1908. Later, he regretted his attempts to seize control of the group, calling the incident "that storm in the Fabian tea-cup."[43]

For six years, through his writings, lectures, and dealings with the Fabians, Wells crusaded for social reforms. These activities took up more of his time, and consequently he spent less time at home. He also began seeing other women when he was away from home in London and other cities. He became increasingly absorbed in his own interests and desires and did not seem to worry about how Jane might be affected. Some of his closest friends felt that success had made him overconfident and insensitive. Shaw scolded him, calling him reckless and lecturing him that being famous did not mean he could say, write, and do whatever he pleased. But Wells did not listen. In spite of his great powers of prediction, he did not foresee that his overconfidence would soon get him into trouble, both privately and publicly.

5 Stirring Up Controversy

The years from 1907 to 1912 were worrisome and upsetting for H.G. Wells. He underwent both personal crisis and public scandal, all as results of his own actions. He had become selfish about his personal relationships, especially his romantic ones. Although he wanted and enjoyed the advantages of a stable home life with one woman, Wells wanted more. Jane cared for

From 1907 to 1908, Wells traveled a good deal of the time. He is photographed here with an associate as they leave a convention in Geneva, Switzerland.

the children, maintained the house, threw parties for their friends, and encouraged him in his work. He loved her for this but had a physical and personal magnetism that easily attracted other women. Wells became increasingly distracted by these relationships and spent less time with his wife and their children. This deeply hurt Jane and almost ruined their marriage.

During this period, some of Wells' ideas were becoming more radical and less socially acceptable. This was especially true of his ideas about sexual freedom. At the time, the strict moral codes associated with the Victorian era were still in effect. Among these were formal dress codes that called for women to cover themselves from neck to ankles. Women were expected to ride horses sidesaddle, keep their legs together when sitting, and refrain from drinking, smoking, and swearing. In addition, most people did not accept the idea of women asking men out, having their own careers, or being the breadwinners in their families. Such behavior was considered overly aggressive and improper for women. Furthermore, women who had children out of wedlock were denounced as immoral.

Wells believed that men and women should be treated as equals and that society should afford women the same privileges as

Women during England's Victorian era were considered properly dressed only when covered from neck to ankles. Wells' forward views on the equality of women and sexual freedom offended Victorian sensibilities.

men. He incorporated these beliefs into his books in an age when most people were not ready to accept them. Many readers thought he was advocating immoral behavior, and his career teetered on the brink of ruin.

Jane's Difficulties

Dissatisfied with her lot in life, Jane became increasingly lonely and unhappy. In 1907 and 1908, Wells was away from Spade House most of the time. Jane knew he was seeing other women but did not object for fear of losing him. When he *was* home, his kidney often acted up, making him irritable and hard to live with. And Jane's everyday routine was difficult. Not only was she

expected to keep up with and try to meet her husband's many needs, but she was also expected to help manage the family finances, act as an efficient housekeeper and hostess, and bring up the children. The boys, then aged seven and five, felt Wells' absence as much as she did. "Gip has three theories about you," she wrote to him. "'Dadda coming,' 'Dadda gone away,' 'Dada asleep'!"[44]

Jane tried reaching out to her husband. On several occasions, she attempted to make him understand what she was going through. For example, after he had been away in London for several weeks, she wrote:

I feel tonight so tired of playing wife making the home comfy & as if there was only one dear rest place in the

Jane Wells with sons Frank and Gip. Wells' absence from home caused his family much emotional distress.

world, & that were in the arms and heart of you. . . . I am thinking continually of the disappointing mess . . . [I am in] . . . the home & furniture & a lot of clothes & books & gardens & a load dragging me down. If I set out to make a comfortable home for you . . . I merely succeed in contriving [creating] a place where you are bored to death. . . . I've had so much of my own society [company] now & I am very naturally getting sick of such a person as I am.[45]

Wells felt guilty and frustrated that things were not right at home. But he refused to alter his busy routine or stop seeing other women. He took Jane for granted, assuming she would always be there for him no matter what he did. Instead of changing his ways, he chose to vent his growing frustrations in his writing. *Kipps* had been a thinly disguised account of his own early life. Because he was, by his own admission, self-centered, writing about himself in the novel had made him feel better. Now, with his spirits low, he embarked upon another novel with a main character much like himself.

Creating a Masterpiece

The new book was *Tono-Bungay,* the story of George Ponderevo, who rises from the working classes of industrial England and finds a better life. He becomes a writer and a socialist and finally aids in the restructuring of society. "It is the most autobiographical of all . . . [Wells'] novels," observed Lovat Dickson. "It recounts in beautiful detail not only his childhood days below-stairs at Up Park, but his period . . . as an apprentice . . . his student days in London, his falling in love with his cousin, his marriage, and the unhappy outcome. George Ponderevo is H.G. Wells not only in the incidental details of his life, but in the expression of his views."[46]

Tono-Bungay was published in 1909 and immediately became successful. Most critical reviews praised the book. Some called it Wells' finest novel, an opinion that has endured among literary experts to the present. Like *Kipps, Tono-Bungay* did not bring about social reform. But readers found George Ponderevo's success story both fascinating and inspiring, and the book sold briskly.

Nature Without Humans

One of Wells' most popular stories was "The Empire of the Ants." In the following excerpt, Wells captures the sharp contrast between natural wilderness and areas colonized and developed by humans. A traveler looks out on the vast, untamed Amazon jungle.

"It was the inhuman immensity of this land that astonished and oppressed him. He knew the skies were empty of men, the stars were specks in an incredible vastness of space; he knew the ocean was enormous and untamable, but in England he had come to think of the land as man's. In England it is indeed man's, the wild things live by sufferance [human permission] . . . everywhere the roads, the fences, and absolute security run. In an atlas too, the land is man's, and all coloured to show his claim to it—in vivid contrast to the universal independent blueness of the sea. He had taken it for granted that a day would come when everywhere about the earth, plough and culture, light tramways [railroads], and good roads, and ordered security would prevail. But now, he doubted."

A Moment of Crisis

No sooner had Wells finished *Tono-Bungay* than he began another novel about contemporary British society. But the new book, titled *Ann Veronica,* did not bring the personal satisfaction and public approval Wells desired. In fact, although it was an excellent novel, *Ann Veronica* represented one of the lowest, most distressful periods of Wells' life. While he was writing it, one of the women he had been seeing became pregnant. There was a terrible scandal. Jane was extremely upset but, as usual, stood by her husband in this moment of crisis. However, many of their friends and acquaintances did not. Many people stopped inviting Wells and Jane to their homes, and some made ugly remarks about Wells behind his back. For this and other reasons he and Jane decided to sell Spade House. They felt that a change of atmosphere in a different part of the country would help them to cope with their embarrassment. In May 1909, they bought a lovely old home in Hampstead, a few miles south of London.

Wells apologized to Jane many times in the following months. He finally seemed to realize how painful his recent behavior had been for her. When she forgave him, he saw how much she loved him, and his love for her became stronger than ever. Later, he recalled her

patience, courage and sacrifice . . . her sense of fair play and perfect generosity. . . . She never told a lie. She managed to sustain her belief that I was worth living for. . . . She stuck to me so sturdily that in the end I stuck to myself. I do not know what I should have been without her. She stabilized my life. She gave me a home and dignity. She preserved its continuity [continued existence].[47]

Breaking the Barrier of Women's Liberation

Although he had come to terms with Jane and his private life, Wells soon found his public life marred by an even larger scandal. It revolved around the contents of *Ann Veronica*. In this book, Wells used his main character to explore an expanded role for women. At the time, most men, and even many women, thought that women should be only wives and mothers. They should not have careers, get involved in politics, or even have the right to vote.

In the novel, Ann Veronica is a beautiful, clever young woman who refuses to obey the dictates of her father and society. She leaves home, borrows money from an older man, and takes a room by herself in London. She then joins the Fabian Society and demonstrates in the streets for women's right to vote. This lands her in jail. Once released, she falls in love with a married man, becomes pregnant, and runs away with him to Switzerland. As usual, Wells' goal was to make people think and to inspire social change. He tried to make the point that Ann's rebellious nature and controversial actions were justified. It was, Wells suggested, society's unfair treatment of women that motivated her. He wanted his readers to acknowledge the widespread repression of women and start treating them better.

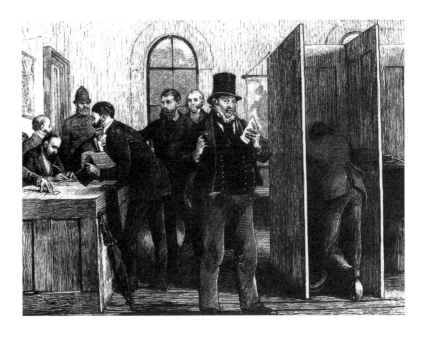

A drawing depicts men voting in a nineteenth-century English election. Women were not allowed to vote. Wells' 1909 novel Ann Veronica *addressed the issue of women's equality and stirred up considerable controversy.*

Wells objected to the narrowness of Victorian morality, which restricted women to the roles of wife, mother, and homemaker.

But the reactions to the novel, both public and private, were far from what Wells had expected. Trouble began immediately after Wells sent the manuscript to his publisher, Frederick Macmillan. On October 19, 1909, Macmillan informed Wells in a letter:

> I regret that we cannot publish *Ann Veronica* as it seems to me a very well written book and there is a great deal in it that is attractive, but the plot develops on lines that would be exceedingly distasteful to the public which buys books published by our firm. The early part of the book with the picture of middle class suburban life is very entertaining. . . . When, however, Ann Veronica begins her pursuit of the Professor . . . and almost forces herself into his arms, the story ceases to be amusing. . . . I can't help thinking that all this part of the story is a mistake and the moral of the book, if there is one, is not such as will commend itself to the majority of the people.[48]

Wells was furious, feeling that Macmillan had abandoned him out of unreasonable fear. He turned to Fisher Unwin, a small publisher who had never before dealt with an author of Wells' stature. Unwin needed a successful book to make his reputation and took a chance on *Ann Veronica.* He was not disappointed. The book proved highly controversial, as Macmillan had predicted, but the controversy only boosted sales.

Polluting the Moral Atmosphere

Although the novel was a financial success, for Wells it was a critical nightmare. Readers and critics alike thought it was scandalous and immoral. Priests and ministers denounced the book in their sermons. One minister, the Reverend Herbert Bull, took up a collection to be used to publish warnings urging people not to read the novel. The president of the Young Women's Christian Association, or YWCA, lectured members that the book was evil and poisonous. Literary reviews echoed the one that appeared in the widely read *Spectator* magazine:

> The loathing [hatred] . . . the book inspires in us is due to the effect it is likely to have in undermining [discouraging] . . . self-control in the individual. . . . It teaches, in effect, that there is no such thing as woman's honour. . . . Such things [as decency and self-restraint] have no place in the muddy world of Mr. Wells's imaginings.[49]

Yielding to Animal Yearning

During the controversy over Wells' book Ann Veronica, *he was criticized and condemned by many groups and individuals. One of the most vocal critics of the book was the popular magazine* Spectator, *which editorialized in November 1909:*

"The loathing [hatred] and indignation [anger] which the book inspires in us are due to the effect it is likely to have in undermining that sense of continence [refraining from sex] and self-control in the individual which is essential in a sound and healthy State. It teaches, in effect, that there is no such thing as woman's honour, or if there is, it is only to be a bulwark [barrier] against a weak temptation [to have sex]. When the temptation is strong enough [Mr. Wells suggests], not only is the tempted person justified in yielding but such yielding becomes not merely inevitable but something to be welcomed and glorified. If an animal yearning or lust is only sufficiently absorbing, it is to be obeyed. Self-sacrifice is a dream and self-restraint a delusion. Such things have no place in the muddy world of Mr. Wells's imaginings. His is a community of scuffling stoats and ferrets [animals that breed quickly], unenlightened by a ray of duty or abnegation [self-denial]."

The *Spectator* also printed a letter from a librarian, who said:

> It has been my duty on several occasions to report certain works of fiction . . . as unfit for circulation, and . . . they have . . . been condemned to be burnt. In the case of *Ann Veronica* . . . how are we to hinder all this literary filth passing into the hands and minds of the public, and thereby polluting the moral atmosphere of our home life?[50]

Wells was perplexed by all this public outrage. At first, he thought his career might be ruined, but when the book sold well he became more amused than worried. He found humor in the fact that so many people rushed out and bought a book that had been so widely denounced as immoral. Wells thought it silly to make such a fuss over what he considered a relatively tame story. There were many women in England in circumstances like Ann's

and he expected everyone to be as open-minded and sympathetic toward them as he was. Besides he thought he had created a vivid, strong, and likable main character. Modern critics have confirmed this opinion, calling *Ann Veronica* one of Wells' best novels. His powers of description are at their peak in the book, as in the following charming portrait of Ann herself. She was, he wrote, a young woman with

> black hair, fine eyebrows, and a clear complexion; and the forces that had modelled her features had loved and lingered at their work and made them subtle and fine. She was slender, and sometimes she seemed tall, and walked and carried herself lightly and joyfully. . . . Her lips came together with an expression between contentment and the faintest shadow of a smile . . . and behind this mask she was wildly discontented and eager for freedom and life.[51]

Wells at work on one of his many manuscripts. His novels depicting liberated women sold well but were denounced as immoral by his contemporaries.

The public outcry against Wells and his writing continued with his next few works, especially *The New Machiavelli,* which was published in 1911. It was another semi-autobiographical story about a social reformer who was trying to better society. As in *Ann Veronica,* there were frank descriptions of liberated women. Also like *Ann Veronica, The New Machiavelli* was condemned by most reviewers but sold exceedingly well.

But interest is not acceptance. Wells learned a lesson from the way people reacted to these books. He realized that society was not yet ready to accept equality for women. He decided to pour his energies into political reform instead, the kind he had experimented with in his utopian books. He would continue to emphasize women's liberation, but only as part of the larger picture of a changing society. After 1912, he no longer wrote traditional novels about everyday life. His books must have a higher purpose, he believed. They must preach nothing less than the restructuring of governments and society and the creation of a better world.

Chapter

6 Toward a New World Order

Between 1912 and 1919, H.G. Wells' writings took a major change of direction. For several years, he had tried to express his ideas in realistic novels about contemporary life. *Kipps, Tono-Bungay,* and *Ann Veronica* had all been attempts to comment

Wells complained to novelist Henry James (below) that the traditional novel could not adequately convey Wells' ideas about changing the world.

on society's ills by showing the struggles of everyday people. Now, Wells decided to abandon this approach. He returned to the more fantastic, future-oriented form of his earlier utopian writings.

Wells made this change because he felt that the traditional type of novel could not get across his larger ideas about changing the world. He believed that conventional novels like those of his friend Henry James had only one main purpose—to entertain. Wells wanted his books to do more. As he wrote to James, "There is of course a fundamental difference in our . . . attitudes towards life and literature. To you literature, like painting, is an end." That is, it diverts people and makes them feel better. "To me," explained Wells, "literature, like architecture, is a means, it has a use."[52]

A Noble Use for the Novel

The use for literature, in Wells' eyes, was to force society to change. He felt such an ambitious task called for books with less realistic, more heroic characters. They would be superior individuals who would express his own philosophy and set an example for readers. By placing these characters in more exaggerated, ideal, futuristic settings, he could show readers the improved world he envisioned. As in his earlier utopian books, Wells' future societies would all have ideal, socialist political systems. He hoped his new works would succeed, where the others had failed, in inspiring his readers to work for a world run by fairer, more ethical governments.

By today's standards, Wells' attempt to bring about major social reform simply by writing books makes him appear to be a hopeless idealist. But in the context of his own time, it seemed a possible, although admittedly very difficult, goal. At the beginning of the twentieth century, the concept of the mass media was still unknown. So works by writers like Wells were often the center of public thought and attention. As the Mackenzies point out:

> Successful writers at this time were "stars," as much in the public eye as film stars and then television personalities became in later years. They made news, and they commented on news, and they were printed whether their opinions were trivial or portentous [important]. Arnold Bennett, indeed, remarked that an eminent [famous] novelist should take care that some newspaper mentioned him every day. The appearance of a series of articles by Wells in the *Daily Mail* [a widely read newspaper] in the middle of May 1912 was one indication of his changing status. He was now sought after as a commentator on social problems and great events.[53]

Wells believed that if he worked hard and long enough, this fame would enable him to reach and influence enough people to bring about social and political change.

A War to End War

In the fateful period between 1912 and 1914, Wells felt that such change was needed more than ever. The world was on the verge of a disastrous war. Relations between the major powers, Britain, France, Germany, and Russia, were rapidly deteriorating. There had been countless wars in the past, but they had been regional conflicts involving only a few nations. By contrast, the impending struggle threatened to engulf the entire world. Many people predicted it would bring about the end of civilization. For nearly two decades, Wells had warned of a major catastrophe for humanity, and now such a disaster actually loomed on the horizon.

This illustration depicts a scene from one of Wells' works about a great war. Years before World War I, Wells had described the horrors of such a war. He sensed war was near but believed humanity would act to prevent it.

A U.S. Army photo captures the growing mushroom cloud of the first atomic bomb test. H.G. Wells had foreseen and described such a weapon decades earlier.

Wells had even foreseen the basic circumstances that led up to World War I. He had described hauntingly similar scenes of European armies mobilizing for battle in his novel *In the Days of the Comet.* And he had discussed the possibility of such a conflict in many other writings. But he had always hoped that the "Great War" would remain fictional. "I will confess," he later recalled, "I saw long ahead how it would happen, and wove fantastic stories about it. I let my imagination play about it, but at the bottom of my heart I could not feel and believe it would really be let happen."[54]

Believing that the war would be disastrous, Wells wrote an article warning of the coming conflict. He called it "The War That Will End War." The war would be so devastating, he suggested, that humanity would either be annihilated or finally learn that fighting is useless. The article was widely read in Britain, France, and the United States, and the title quickly became the slogan most people used in referring to the war. Wells later expanded the article into a book with the same title and theme.

The World State

In 1913, Wells realized that the conflict was probably inevitable. Germany had built up a huge army and threatened to invade France. Britain and most other nations were sure to be drawn into the struggle. It was too late for writers like him to appeal to reason and sway the great powers from their disastrous course. But perhaps, Wells thought, some good might come out of the conflict. As he had suggested in "The War That Will End War," maybe humanity would be shocked by its own barbarity and learn its lesson. It might rise from the ashes and finally build the ideal, utopian society he advocated.

For months, Wells devoted most of his energies to writing *The World Set Free.* It was one of his grandest attempts to point the way to a better future. And it stands as one of the best examples of his utopian writing. In this book, Wells used most of the major themes that characterize this branch of his work. One of these themes was that war might be a means of cleansing the world of its old evils. After the slate had been wiped clean, the way would be clear for new and better ideas and institutions.

The most original theme in the book was the idea of a world government. The concept of nations, Wells felt, was old-fashioned and dangerous. It led only to rivalries, bickering, and wars like the one about to be fought. A single, all-powerful government for the whole globe, Wells proposed, would eliminate national boundaries and the troubles that go with them.

Wells proposed that this government be ruled by a group of "enlightened" leaders. Rather than being obsessed with wealth and power, they would be teachers and scientists who were interested only in constructive pursuits. These were the same "capable men" Wells had mentioned in his earlier utopian works. Under their leadership, people would build what Wells called a "new world order." In this order, everyone would have equal opportunities. There would be no poverty because the government would help the needy. Since all of people's material needs would be met, presumably there would be no crime. There would also be complete freedom of expression and no one would be punished for expressing an opinion. In addition, women would enjoy complete equality with men. Women would not feel that their only role in life is to get married and have children.

Inventing the Ultimate Weapon

Wells constructed the plot of *The World Set Free* to illustrate all of these ideas. He set the opening scenes of the book in the middle of the twentieth century, describing a horrendous world war that almost destroys humanity. Without realizing it, he was predicting the ravages of World War II before the first world war had even been fought.

The Japanese city of Hiroshima was flattened by an atomic bomb blast in 1945. World War II brought many of the terrors Wells described in his story of a final, great war that would end all wars.

Physicist Leo Szilard explains atomic reactions to a congressional committee in the early 1940s. Szilard had read Wells' book about future atomic destruction, and it had made him uneasy about developing an atomic bomb.

The weapon that causes most of the destruction in Wells' fictional war is an atomic bomb. When he envisioned this weapon, its actual invention was still nearly thirty years away. No one knew yet that a chain reaction of atomic particles splitting atoms apart could release vast amounts of energy. By skillfully combining his strong background in science and his vivid imagination, Wells made a brilliant guess about the powers of the atom. The result was a remarkably accurate picture of what such a device would be like. In the book, he described how humanity is so horrified by the weapon that people swear never to use it again. Thus, Wells also anticipated the real reaction to the U.S. bombing of Hiroshima and Nagasaki in Japan during World War II. Since the 1940s, the fear of total destruction has kept nations that possess nuclear weapons from actually using them.

Wells' description of the atomic bomb had later consequences that he did not

foresee when he wrote *The World Set Free.* One of the scientists who developed the bomb, Leo Szilard, read the book in 1933. Szilard claimed that Wells influenced his work on nuclear chain reactions, which began a year later. The terrible consequences of a bomb such as that described in the book frightened Szilard. "Knowing what this would mean—and I knew it because I had read H.G. Wells," Szilard later wrote, "I did not want this . . . [idea] to become public."[55]

In *The World Set Free,* after the final war, a new age begins. Wells called it the Rule of the Saints. His "capable men" have been living in the remote Himalayan Mountains, untouched by the destruction that has swept the world. They emerge and begin teaching the survivors how to start over. The idea of a handful of people preserving civilization in the Himalayas of Asia strongly influenced other writers. The best-known example was James Hilton, whose novel *Lost Horizon* used the same concept. In Wells' book, after the new world order becomes reality, humanity turns toward the heavens and the challenge of space travel. Says Karenin, the story's main character:

We can still keep our feet upon the earth that made us. But the air no longer imprisons us, this round planet is no longer chained to us like the ball of a galley-slave. . . . In a little while men who will know how to bear the different gravitations, the altered pressures, the attenuated [thin] unfamiliar gases and all the fearful strangeness of space will be venturing out from this earth. This ball will be no longer enough for us; our spirit will reach out. . . . Cannot you see how that little argosy [spacecraft] will go glittering up into the sky, twinkling and glittering smaller and smaller until the blue swallows it up? They may succeed out there; they may perish, but other men will follow them. It is as if a great window opened . . .[56]

Criticizing Shaw

Following the outbreak of World War I in 1914, Wells published several articles urging the establishment of a new world order at the war's end. This irritated some of Wells' literary friends, including Shaw, who wrote articles taking exception to some of Wells' statements. Following is an excerpt from one of Wells' articles rebutting Shaw that appeared in the December 31, 1914 issue of the Daily Chronicle.

"Mr. Shaw objects to my calling him muddleheaded. But I have always considered him muddleheaded. If I have not called him that in public before, it is simply because I thought the thing too obvious to need pointing out. If we see a man making an ass of himself, we indolent [lazy] English accept him rather than face the boring task of pursuing him into the recesses of his unsoundness [stupidity]. . . . And that is how things stand between Mr. Shaw and myself. . . . Mr. Shaw is one of those perpetual children who live in a dream of make-believe, and the make-believe of Mr. Shaw is that he is a person of incredible wisdom and subtlety running the world. He is an elderly adolescent still at play. . . . How are we to gather together the wills and understanding of men for the tremendous necessities and opportunities of the time?. . . There is work for every man who writes or talks, and has the slightest influence upon another creature. All the slaughter [of the war] is only a darkness of the mind. It goes on only because we who are [influential] voices . . . are ourselves such little scattered creatures that . . . we still have no strength that would turn on the light [find the way] that would save us."

British soldiers defend a war-torn piece of territory during World War I. Wells' writings focused on the development of a new world order after the war.

Wells used the idea of moving into space in other utopian books, most notably *The Shape of Things to Come.* His vision of the "final frontier" for humanity clearly foreshadowed the real exploration of outer space that began in the 1960s.

Knowledge—the Key to the Future

As Wells expected, the Great War began in 1914. The next few years were difficult and fearful for the people of Britain. Thousands of young British men were dying in the trenches in Europe. And there was constant worry that Germany might invade the British Isles. Wells and Jane tried their best to keep up their own spirits, as well as those of their friends. On weekends, they threw large parties that a friend described as "whirls of unceasing activity." The festivities went on from early morning until late evening and included lawn tennis, field hockey, dancing, card games, and lively discussions.

But during the weekdays, Wells was a different man. He concentrated on what he saw as a serious matter—the direction humanity would take after the war. *The World Set Free* had sold well. Interpreting this as proof that people wanted to hear his ideas, he followed it up with more utopian tales in the same vein. These included *War and the Future, Mr. Britling Sees It Through,* and *What Is Coming: A Forecast of Things After the War.*

In each of these works, Wells preached about the new world order and predicted that knowledge was the key to the future. He foresaw humanity using science as a tool to lift the veil of darkness that hides nature's mysteries. To him, it was that same darkness that surrounded the man holding the lit match in the article he had penned so long ago, "The Rediscovery of the Unique." Each new discovery, he had said, would reveal that a multitude of mysteries remained undetected. Now at the height of his powers as a writer, he described this idea again. In one of his most famous utopian books, *Men Like Gods,* a member of an advanced race addresses an ordinary human:

> We have gone on for three thousand years now, and a hundred million good brains have been put like grapes into the wine-press of science. And we know today—how little we know. There is never an observation made but a hundred observations are missed in the making of it. . . . We have forms of expression that we cannot get over [explain] to you so that things that used to seem difficult . . . to you, lose all their difficulty in our minds. . . . Our minds have exceeded [gone beyond] our lives. . . . We are like little children who have been brought to the shores of a limitless ocean. All the knowledge we have gathered . . . is like a small handful of pebbles gathered upon the shore of that limitless sea. . . . Some day you [humanity] too will become again like little children, and . . . [we] will be waiting for you. Two universes will embrace, to beget a yet greater universe. . . . And it will be no more than a beginning, no more than a beginning.[57]

Disappointment

Wells' readers did not take these tales of advanced races and future science seriously. Once again, they saw his stories purely as pleasant and fascinating entertainment. His books inspired no army of reformers clamoring for a new world order based on equality, peaceful endeavors, and

---

"Literature Is Illumination"

During the war, Wells wrote Boon, *the story of a writer, much like himself, who turned out popular works but longed to write great literature that moves the masses. In the following excerpt from the book,* Boon, *the main character, explains the importance of literature to humanity.*

"If all the world went frantic; if presently [soon afterward] some horrible thing, some monstrous war, smashed all books and thinking and civilization, still the mind would be there. It would immediately go on again and presently it would pick up [rediscover] all that had been done before—just as a philosopher would presently go on reading again after the servant-girl had fallen downstairs with the crockery. It is the Mind of the Race [the human race]. Most of the race is out of touch with it, lost to it. Much of the race is talking and doing nonsense and cruelty; astray, absurd. That does not matter to the truth. . . . It matters to Literature. It matters because Literature, the clearing of minds, the release of minds, the food and guidance of minds, is the way, Literature is illumination, the salvation of ourselves, and everyone."

Norwegian officials join an international group in England after World War I to establish the League of Nations. Wells had called for such an organization years earlier, but after the war he believed that a one world government should be established.

the endless pursuit of knowledge. Wells was also disappointed that at war's end in 1918 there was little indication that humanity would change its ways. The world's armies had grown larger than ever and nation still threatened nation. Yet there *was* one hopeful sign. The war's victors organized the League of Nations, an international group designed to settle disputes among countries. Wells had argued for founding such a group for many years. But now he believed that the league was not enough. It seemed to only reinforce the idea of individual nations, and he wanted to see a world state emerge.

Frustrated, Wells tried desperately to explain why people and nations seemed so unwilling to institute change. And then he hit upon what he believed was the answer. People did not respond to his ideas in literature, he theorized, because they were too ignorant about history. They did not grasp that war and misery were part of a pattern that constantly repeated itself. If they could see and appreciate this fact, his preachings would have more meaning. People would then rise up and break this destructive pattern. Now, with unbounded enthusiasm, Wells took upon himself yet another difficult task—the education of the masses. He had begun as a teacher of children. He would now become a teacher of the entire human race.

7 History as Teacher

H.G. Wells was thoroughly disillusioned with the aftermath of World War I. The war had been devastating, as he had predicted. But it had not produced a new world order as he had hoped. And the League of Nations was far from what Wells had expected or hoped for as a world organization. He wanted the league to begin the task of erasing national boundaries in preparation for a world state. He quickly saw that the organization was a nearly useless body that could barely settle minor disputes among nations. He began referring to world leaders, many of whom he knew personally, as "uneducated blockheads."

Wells experienced another disappointment at war's end. In 1917, the Russian Communists, led by Vladimir Lenin, had overthrown the monarchy of Czar Nicholas II. Lenin and his followers promised to institute a fair and equitable socialist state. At first, Wells thought that Russia might be the birthplace of a new world order. The Russians might set an example for the rest of the world and the idea might spread. He decided to visit Russia to see firsthand the extent of social change. As Lovat Dickson explains:

> Wells was a famous man even in this starving, fearful land of revolutionary Russia . . . immersed in its own troubles. . . . [Wells] was invited to address the Petrograd Soviet [a local ruling body]. . . . [Later] he made the journey to Moscow to see Lenin. Wells

Russian leader Vladimir Lenin addresses a crowd in Moscow's Red Square in 1919. H.G. Wells visited with Lenin to discuss political theory but was disappointed with Lenin's ideas.

was all seriousness, questioning Lenin closely about the present mentality [thinking] on which he must rebuild his shattered nation. But Lenin discoursed [spoke] on practical notions about restoring the economy through... [providing electric power for] industry ... and did not show much interest in theoretical ideas about education.[58]

Though disappointed with Lenin's ideas, Wells hoped that a new world order still might take root in Russia. But he soon saw this dream evaporate. He was appalled when Communist rule in Russia became just another form of dictatorship.

A New Sort of History

In addition to disappointments about Russia and the League of Nations, Wells had to contend with what he saw as his own failure in the war years. His books had not stirred people's hearts as he had hoped. In

---

The Ice Age

Much of Wells' non-fiction is as colorful and descriptive as his fiction. Here, from The Outline of History, *he describes the ages that passed on the primitive earth as the ice ages approached.*

"Through millions of animal generations the spinning world circled about the sun; slowly its orbit, which may have been nearly circular during the equable [pleasant] days of the early Eocene, was drawn by the attraction of the circulating outer planets into a more elliptical [egg-shaped] form. Its axis of rotation, which heeled over to the plane of its orbit, as the mast of a yacht under sail heels over towards the water, heeled over by imperceptible [too tiny to detect] degrees a little more and a little more. And each year its summer point shifted a little farther.... These were small changes.... They were changes an immortal astronomer in Neptune, watching the earth from age to age, would have found almost imperceptible.... Age by age the winters grew, on the whole, colder and harder and longer relatively to the summers; age by age the summers grew briefer. On an average, the winter snow lay a little later in the spring in each century, and the glaciers in the northern mountains gained an inch this year, receded half an inch next, came on again a few inches.... Then, rather less deliberately ... the ice came on into the temperate [warmer] regions of the earth."

his mind, there seemed only one logical explanation of why the public did not get his message. People just did not understand their own past. They did not grasp, as he did, that destructive political systems and corrupt leaders constantly repeated the same mistakes. If enough powerful and influential people had realized this, he believed, World War I might never have been fought. He saw the reason for the war as an educational breakdown and expressed the belief that the only hope for humanity lay in education.

Wells decided that he must instruct his readers about history. He believed that they needed to see where the human race had come from in order to understand where they should go. He had tried using politics to instruct, and he had tried creating fictional models in his books. These approaches had not worked. Now, Wells was determined to return to his original profession—teaching. But this time he would be a teacher of the entire human race.

Wells decided that his teaching tool would be a huge book that told the entire history of the earth. "It will be a new sort of history," he explained, "that will twist the minds of its readers round towards a new set of values. There's really nothing more to be done with our present public until its ideas about history are changed."[59] Wells decided to call the book *The Outline of History.* He summed up its central theme and message in a magazine article:

No one has ever attempted to teach our children the history of man . . . with all his early struggles and triumphs . . . his . . . tribes and nations, his conquests of Nature, his creations of Art, his building up of Science. . . . An enormous amount of work has to be done if we are to teach the peoples of the world what is the truth . . . that they are all engaged in a common work, that they have sprung from common origins, and are all contributing some special service to the general end [future].[60]

Creating a Life's Work in a Year

Wells was right when he referred to the work to be done as "enormous." No one had ever before tried to write a comprehensive history covering everything from the formation of the solar system to the present day. Wells hired several researchers and other assistants to help him gather

Jane Wells types up notes for her husband's monumental The Outline of History. *The Wells' sometimes worked fifteen hours a day compiling material for the volume.*

H.G. Wells at the height of his career. A truly gifted writer, Wells was able to produce in one year the work of a lifetime: The Outline of History.

information. Jane became his main assistant. The two put in twelve-to-fifteen-hour days, rarely taking a day off. They pored over hundreds of books, articles, and other references, slowly piecing together the massive manuscript. Often, they worried whether all this effort would pay off. They did not expect to make much money from the book. No history book had ever been a best-seller. But they hoped the copies that did sell would begin to change the way people saw their place in the long pageant of humanity.

Wells finished *The Outline* late in 1919 and it was published a few months later. It was an immense volume—more than 750,000 words in length—ten times longer than the average popular novel. Wells'

friend Arnold Bennett, who read it before it was published, was amazed. "How the fellow did the book in the [short] time," Bennett wrote to Jane, "fair passes [is beyond] me. I cannot get over it. It's a life's work." Bennett was also impressed with the content of the book, saying it was "the most useful thing of the kind ever done, and it is jolly well done."[61]

Critical reviews of *The Outline* mirrored Bennett's comments. Most critics, including many professional historians, praised the book in the highest possible terms. One of the greatest and most respected of all historians, Arnold Toynbee, called *The Outline* "a magnificent intellectual achievement." Toynbee dismissed the few history professors who criticized Wells for meddling in their field. "In re-living the entire life of Mankind as a single

Famed historian Arnold Toynbee praised The Outline of History *as "a magnificent intellectual achievement."*

emotional experience," said Toynbee, "Mr. Wells was achieving something which they [the professors] would hardly have dared to attempt."[62]

In addition to critical praise, *The Outline* also brought financial rewards. This surprised Wells and Jane, as well as the publisher and everyone else connected with the book. Never before had a nonfiction book sold so well. For months, the publisher could not print copies fast enough. And this success continued for several years. By 1925, more than two million copies of *The Outline* had sold in Britain and the United States alone. Even with today's much larger reading public, this would be considered a tremendous success. At that time, it was simply unbelievable. To Wells' amazement, the book sold more copies than all of his other books combined. This made him far wealthier than he had ever imagined he would be. From this point on, he would be able to take on any project he desired and not have to worry about how much money it would make.

Bold, Brilliant, and Exciting

For Wells, the critical and financial success of *The Outline* could not erase the fact that he had once again failed to achieve his primary goal. All through the early and mid-1920s, he waited naïvely for some sign that the book was having an effect on society. But such a sign never appeared. Though many schools used the book and millions of people read it, *The Outline* seemed to have no perceptible impact on society. How could the book sell so well, Wells wondered, and still not move people? The answer, he finally realized, was that it did move people, but not in the way he had hoped it would. As with so many of his other works, people liked the book because it was entertaining. He had managed to turn the history of the world into an exciting, exotic, action-packed, and fascinating story. The following excerpt, describing the Romans laying siege to the city of Carthage, illustrates his storytelling style of teaching:

> There followed the most obstinate [stubborn] and dreadful of sieges. Scipio . . . cut off all supplies by land and sea. The Carthaginians suffered horribly from famine; but they held out until the town was stormed. The street fighting lasted for six days, and when at last the citadel capitulated [surrendered] there were fifty thousand Carthaginians left alive out of an estimated population of half a million. These survivors went into slavery, the whole city was burnt, the ruins were ploughed to express [cause] final destruction, and a curse was invoked [cast] . . . upon anyone who might attempt to rebuild it.[63]

Wells no doubt succeeded in educating many of his readers while entertaining them. But no one saw *The Outline* as an urgent call to reform the world. People thought of it as an unusually good book and nothing more.

Criminal Charges

There was one reader, however, whose reaction to the book upset Wells more than any other. She was a Canadian writer named Florence Deeks. In 1925, she claimed that Wells had plagiarized, or

A drawing depicts the Roman siege of Carthage. Wells' powers as a storyteller made this and other events in history very entertaining reading.

copied, *The Outline of History* from her several years before. According to Deeks, Wells' book was substantially the same as a book she had wanted to publish called *The Web of History.* Deeks and Wells had the same publisher, and she insisted that Wells must have seen her manuscript in the publisher's office and stolen it. The charge was untrue, but Deeks continued to pester Wells for years, bringing him to court on several occasions. It was not until 1932 that the matter was finally settled. As a last resort, Deeks appealed to the king of England and he ruled in Wells' favor.

Though angered about being called a thief, Wells did not let the matter deter him from his work. In the 1920s, he completed several more utopian novels. He also began

writing two more huge educational volumes. They were *The Science of Life: A Summary of Contemporary Knowledge About Life and Its Possibilities* and *The Work, Wealth and Happiness of Mankind.* He intended these as companion volumes to *The Outline of History.* The first would explain the discoveries of science and the other would explain modern political and social institutions. Both books took years to complete. Unfortunately, neither was nearly as popular as *The Outline.* This became still another major disappointment for Wells to bear.

A Soul in Torment

In May 1927, such worries about his books, and all other aspects of his life as well, suddenly seemed trivial and unimportant to Wells. He was staying temporarily in Paris when the news came that Jane had been diagnosed as having cancer. It was an advanced case, and Wells realized that she was doomed. On his way back to England, he wrote to her, "My dear, I love you much more than I have loved anyone else in the world & I am coming back to you to take care of you."[64] For several months, he tried to make her as comfortable as possible. But the disease quickly took its toll.

Jane died on October 6, 1927, at the age of fifty-five. According to friends, Wells seemed to fall apart before their eyes. George Bernard Shaw's wife, Charlotte, later recalled that the funeral

> was dreadful—dreadful—*dreadful!* I haven't been so upset . . . for a long time . . . H.G. began to cry like a child—tried to hide it at first and then let go. . . . It was terrible beyond anything words can describe; a soul in

Jane's Contribution

After Jane's death, Wells looked back on their marriage and her contributions to it. In his autobiography, he finally acknowledged that without her he could not have succeeded so well in his own endeavors.

"I am appalled to reflect how much of the patience, courage and sacrifice of our compromises came from her. . . . We had two important things in our favor, first that we had a common detestation not only of falsehood but of falsity, and secondly, that we had the sincerest affection and respect for each other. There again the feat was hers. It was an easy thing for me to keep my faith in her sense of fair play and her perfect generosity. She never told a lie. To the end I would have taken her word against all the other witnesses in the world. But she managed to sustain her belief that I was worth living for, and that was a harder task, while I made my way through a tangle of moods and impulses [and affairs with other women] that were quite outside her instinctive sympathy. She stuck to me so sturdily that in the end I stuck to myself. I do not know what I should have done without her. She stabilized my life. She gave me a home and dignity. She preserved its continuity."

torment—self-torture. He drowned us in a sea of misery and as we were gasping began . . . [to describe] Jane . . . as a delicate, flower-like, gentle being, surrounding herself with beauty, philanthropy [generosity] and love. . . . H.G. positively howled. . . . O it was hideous—terrible and frightful.[65]

Jane's passing marked a significant turning point in Wells' life. She had provided him with companionship, a stable home, children, and, most important, a deep and unselfish love. Now, there was a void in his life that he sensed no one else would be able to fill. He also felt a terrible guilt over the times he had hurt her or taken her for granted. Eventually, he returned to his work, and on the surface he seemed his old self. But emotionally, he would never be the same again.

8 The Eternal Optimist

After Jane's death, H.G. Wells slowly began to decline, both physically and mentally. In addition to her loss, he felt increasing frustration with the way the world was going. No new sweeping reforms for humanity appeared on the immediate horizon. But what bothered him even more was his own continuing inability to bring about those

After losing his wife and his readership, the aging Wells fought a growing bitterness of spirit.

reforms. He still took his ideas about a new world order seriously, but the public did not. Both his readers and his critics became bored with his books, which seemed endlessly to repeat the same ideas and themes. This negative reaction to his work, coupled with his increasing age, made him defensive and irritable.

In this last period of his life, Wells finally began to admit to himself that the great changes he envisioned might not come in his lifetime. He sometimes allowed himself to think that he had spent his life chasing an impossible dream. But deep inside of him, the old H.G., the fighter and idealist, still refused to give up. A part of him was still determined to "live as though it were not so." To the end, Wells remained optimistic that there was hope for humanity. He also hoped that his work would contribute to shaping the new society that he would never see.

The Man Who Invented Tomorrow

An important clue to Wells' growing unhappiness and bitterness appeared in 1936. It was a book titled *The Anatomy of Frustration.* In it, Wells theorized about

A Drive to Make Life Better

Wells' friend Beatrice Webb made a perceptive entry in her diary shortly after Wells published his autobiography in 1934. Her comments give some clue to why he never succeeded in reforming society through his writings.

"In spite of deplorable [rude] literary manners, and mean sexual morals, H.G. is to me a likeable and valuable man. He has been on the side of the angels; he has wanted to make life better for the masses of men and he subordinated [used] his art to that purpose. . . . Except for his admiration for Huxley, Wells grew up with a contempt for his fellow human beings, notably for the existing governing class, on the one hand, and for the multitude of manual workers on the other. . . . But unfortunately Wells has not been satisfied to be a delightful romancer—he has thought of himself as a great thinker—as a shaper of the world to come . . . this grandiose [gigantic] aim needs some knowledge of social institutions—and H.G. Wells is as innocent of this specialized knowledge as I am of the mysteries of mathematics. . . . He did not want to examine the origin, growth, disease and death of social institutions; he wanted to judge them."

Wells' friend Beatrice Webb proved insightful in summing up his personality flaws.

why people were so unwilling to work and sacrifice for change. He suggested that humanity was as frustrated with the condition of the world as he was. In conversations with friends and letters to them, he frequently pondered why people were so frustrated. But *The Anatomy of Frustration?* failed to answer this question. In fact, there were no new explanations, suggestions, or ideas in the book. Wells simply preached, as he had before, that people must cast off the ways of the past. They must seek and utilize new knowledge to build a better society.

Some of Wells' friends offered him an answer to the question he had posed. They suggested that he expected too much from others. He expected everyone else to be as caring, committed, and hardworking as he was. He wanted them to think mainly in terms of the general happiness of humanity. But the average person, Wells' friends said, is more concerned with everyday survival and his or her own happiness. Thus, his expectations of others were unrealistic and bound to cause him disappointment and frustration.

But Wells refused to accept this explanation. He chose instead to fall back on his idea that lack of education was to blame. He was especially critical of schools, which he said produced "hordes of fundamentally ignorant, unbalanced, uncriticical minds. . . . Mere cannon-fodder [waste material] and stuff for massacres and stampedes."[66] He described as followers people who were incapable of thinking for themselves. With so little learning, he insisted, most people did not know what needed changing or how to go about changing it.

He now admitted that a new world order would take longer to build than he had hoped. But he insisted that people would build it eventually and that he must help lay the groundwork. He continued to hammer out utopian books, desperately trying to get his message across. Among these were *Mr. Blettsworthy on Rampole Island, The Holy Terror, The New World Order,* and *The Fate of Homo Sapiens.*

None of these books sold as well as Wells' earlier works, and his reading audience began to shrink. Also, the critics treated him increasingly harshly. They charged that he had nothing new to say, calling his writing boring and repetitious. Many people missed the younger Wells, whose literary voice had been so original and moving. As Norman Mackenzie put it, "He had been one of the first to write about the crisis of world civilization . . . and among the first to discuss the need for an international organization. He had been a spokesman for the creative possibilities of science . . . a champion of a reformed . . . educational system. . . . There was some justice in calling him 'The Man Who Invented Tomorrow.'"[67] But now, Wells was becoming a bitter old man, insisting on delivering the same old message in the same old way.

An Experiment in Staying Awake

Although most of his work repeated old messages, Wells managed to find two new ways to express himself. The first was through writing the story of his own life. Published in 1934, it was titled *Experiment in Autobiography: Discoveries and Conclusions of a Very Ordinary Brain.* Friends such as Shaw and Bennett found his false modesty humorous, for Wells' brain was far from ordinary. Friends called Wells' intellect huge and his personality gigantic. And this unique, larger-than-life personality was evident on every page of the book.

Experiment was no average autobiography. It was the dramatic tale of a man struggling against the tides and trends of history, of a great voice crying out for change. And it moved everyone who read it. The American president, Franklin D. Roosevelt, wrote to Wells, "*Experiment in Autobiography* was for me an experiment in staying awake instead of putting the light out. How do you manage to retain such vivid pictures of events and such extraordinarily clear impressions [of the past]?"[68] One of Wells' friends had been impressed with the way Wells had described his relationships with women in the book. Wells could analyze

President Franklin D. Roosevelt enjoyed reading Wells' autobiography so much that he wrote Wells a fan letter.

women better than anyone else, declared the friend. But despite such praises, *Experiment* had only moderate sales. Because of the preaching and repetition of ideas in his other books, his readers were clearly losing interest in him.

Creating a Marching Song for Humanity

The other new means of expression Wells attempted to use in his final years was that of film. He correctly saw that movies were fast becoming an even more persuasive means of expressing ideas than books. In 1933, he had written a utopian book titled *The Shape of Things to Come: The Ultimate Revolution*. In it, he had vividly summed up his vision of a new world order and predicted the events of the coming 150 years. In 1934, Wells met the famous film designer and director Alexander Korda. Korda convinced Wells to write the script for a film version of *Things to Come*. The director gave the author a free hand, which was unusual in the movie business. Korda felt it was a way of showing respect for one of the great writers of the day.

For months, Wells worked closely with the film company, revising and adding to the script often. The film tells a story of humanity's being devastated by a great war, then rising from the ruins. A group of pilots and scientists, Wells' "capable men," lead the way to a utopian society. In the finale, society stands on the verge of space travel. Wells wanted the ending to fill the audience with pride in the possibility of human achievement. It should be "a shout of human resolution [desire to be better],"

Famed film director Alexander Korda, shown here with his actress wife Merle Oberon, worked with Wells on a film version of Wells' book The Shape of Things to Come.

a "marching song of a new world of conquest among the atoms and stars."[69] Wells succeeded in making the film's finale both dramatic and memorable. As humanity's first two space travelers hurtle into the heavens, the earth's leading scientist delivers a majestic speech. It is one of Wells' purest, most moving expressions of the dignity and destiny of the human race. It is the voice of an eternal optimist:

> There! There they go. . . . What they have done is magnificent. . . . [They will go on] until a landing is made and the moon is conquered. This is only a beginning. . . . Is there ever to be any age of happiness? Is there ever to be any rest? . . . For Man, no rest and no ending. He must go on, conquest beyond conquest. First, this little planet . . . and then all the laws of mind and matter that restrain him, then the planets about him. And at last, out across immensity to the stars. And when he has conquered all the deeps of space and all the mysteries of time, still he will be beginning. . . . It is . . . all the universe or nothing. Which shall it be? *Which shall it be?*[70]

The futuristic sets, costumes, and special effects in *Things to Come* made the film fascinating to watch. Unfortunately, these were the only things that most audiences and critics liked about the film. They found Wells' story and dialogue, as in his books, too much of a lecture on the way the world ought to be. The characters, they said, seemed constantly to preach at the audience. Suffering still another disappointment, Wells bitterly lashed out, blaming Korda and others rather than himself for the film's shortcomings.

Throughout his illustrious career H.G. Wells used words to fight for a new world order—a fight he never won.

The Time Traveller's Journey Ends

At the end of their biography The Time Traveller, *the Mackenzies movingly sum up Wells' contributions to humanity. They begin by quoting from writer J.B. Priestley's remarks delivered at Wells' funeral service. They then describe Wells' last resting place.*

"J.B. Priestley bade farewell to 'the great prophet of our time.' . . . For Priestley, as for so many others who had enjoyed all that was best in H.G., there was also a warmer memory of 'the man who could write *Kipps* and *Tono-Bungay,* the man who could enrich his letters with droll little drawings . . . whose blue eyes twinkled with mischief . . . who was not only a tremendous character but also a most lovable man. . . . When he was angry, it was because he knew, far better than we did, that life need not be a sordid greedy scramble; and when he was impatient it was because he knew there were glorious gifts of body, mind and spirit only just beyond our present reach.' Priestley had spoken for the generations who felt that Wells had been their spokesman, giving himself to a great vision [of bettering the world] and martyring himself [devoting his life] in its service. . . . No other man spanning the years between [Darwin's] *The Origin of the Species* and the Hiroshima bomb, had so faithfully mirrored the dualism [contrast between good and evil] of his own kind or demonstrated better the conflict of the divided self that could not accept the human condition. Gip Wells and Anthony West took the ashes of their father down to the Isle of Wight and scattered them over the sea. The journey of the Time Traveller was over."

At Wells' funeral service, writer J.B. Priestley praised Wells' character and career.

Fighting the Odds

Wells' bitterness about his work and the state of the world only increased as the years went on. He refused to listen to criticism, even from friends, that his books had become huge, rambling, boring lectures. His last few works, such as *The Outlook for Homo Sapiens* and *Mind at the End of Its Tether*, were typical examples. Aging, disappointed, and without Jane's comfort and companionship, Wells became increasingly unhappy. His health began to fail, too. His kidney ailment reappeared and he contracted neuritis, a nerve disease. It made him irritable and often interfered with his writing. His friend Beatrice Webb lunched with him and later sadly recalled how both his mind and body had deteriorated:

> He was at work summing up the human race as a species of animal, living on this planet. Would it survive and progress, or would it die out like other species had done, because it could not adapt itself to changing environment? . . . I found him a physical wreck. . . . He was obsessed with his own vague vision of a world order. . . .

But he utterly failed to make me understand what sort of social institution he had in mind. . . . He rejected all those existing; he insisted that his organ of government must represent and govern the world at large. . . . Poor old Wells—I was sorry for him. I doubt whether we shall meet again—we are [both] too old and tired.[71]

Yet occasionally, Wells managed to express himself clearly. When he did, he voiced his undying optimism for humanity's future. His old determination to "live as though it were not so" surfaced once more. "I think the odds are against man," he said near the end of his life, "but it is still worth fighting against them."[72]

For Wells, that noble fight ended on Thursday, August 13, 1946. In the afternoon, he told his nurse he wanted to take a nap and dismissed her. He died in his sleep at 4:15 P.M. at the age of seventy-nine.

In his writing, his voice had given life to the Time Traveler and the Invisible Man, to Artie Kipps and Ann Veronica, to common folk and godlike beings. Now, that great voice that had cried out so tirelessly for a better world was still at last.

9 A Mighty Imagination

Although H.G. Wells was a well-known figure when he was alive, the major impact his works had on literature, the mass media, and society came later, after his death. Wells had desperately wanted to make an impact in his own lifetime. For decades he had waited naïvely for his writings to stir public passions and help bring about major social and political changes in the world. But he was continually disappointed. Humanity was not yet ready for his idealistic solutions to its problems. But Wells refused to accept this and blamed himself for what he considered his failure to make an impact. "My epitaph [words on tombstone]," he said, "will be 'He was clever, but not clever enough . . . '"[73] He went to his grave believing that he had failed in his quest to help shape the future.

The Literature of Change

Wells did have an important impact on the future, but in a different way from what he had foreseen. Today, he is considered, along with French writer Jules Verne, one of the two originators of science fiction. This is the branch of fiction that deals with the possibilities of science and its impact on human beings. Many of Wells' works,

especially his scientific romances and short stories, are looked upon now as science fiction classics.

Of course, Wells had no idea when he wrote these works that they would help create a new literary field. In fact, that field, including the term *science fiction* itself, did not exist until the 1920s. In 1926, American writer and editor Hugo Gernsback began publishing the magazine *Amazing*. The stories that appeared in *Amazing* were

Together with H.G. Wells, Jules Verne (below) is credited as one of the originators of science fiction.

Modern master of science fiction Isaac Asimov and two robots promote Asimov's science fiction video game. Asimov credited H.G. Wells with laying the groundwork for every science fiction theme developed by later writers.

mainly weird or fantastic tales that revolved around scientific concepts. At first, Gernsback published reprints of old stories by Wells, Jules Verne, Edgar Allen Poe, and other great writers. Soon, however, he began hiring young, unknown writers who turned out stories vividly depicting such future inventions as robots, computers, satellites, and atomic weapons.

Although Wells did not mind making money from the reprints of his old stories, he never wrote any new material for *Amazing* or any of the similar publications that followed it. To him, most of the stories in these publications were trivial, poorly written, and appealed to people with little education. He felt he was a great writer whose work had an important message. But, without realizing it, Wells contributed to early science fiction indirectly, by inspiring and influencing young science fiction writers. For example, the first science fiction stories dealing with atomic bombs owed their ideas to Wells' invention of the concept in *The World Set Free*.

Eventually, after Wells' death, science fiction became a more respected art form and attracted many gifted writers. The audience for science fiction grew to tens of millions as more and more people realized that science was bringing about swift and dramatic changes in the world. No other branch of literature seemed to explore these changes and their impact on human beings. Because science fiction did consider the possibilities of the future, the field became known as the literature of change. As noted writer Isaac Asimov put it, "Science fiction is based on the fact of social change. It accepts the fact of change. In a sense, it tries on various changes for size; it tries to penetrate the consequences of this change or that; and, in the form of a story, it presents the results to the view of the public."[74] Because it helps people understand the nature of

The Beginning of Modern Science Fiction

In an introduction to Three Novels of the Future, *science fiction master Isaac Asimov explains what Wells taught all the writers of fantastic literature who followed him and points out a Wellsian lesson that still instructs people today. After telling how Wells turned the British upper and lower social classes into the Eloi and Morlocks in* The Time Machine, *Asimov writes:*

"But, mind you, one does not read the novel with the constant awareness of satire. Wells makes so interesting and detailed a story of it that you read it for the story's sake alone, and only afterward—perhaps—consider the lesson. How much deeper the shaft sinks because of the delayed reaction and how much less likely you are to forget it. Science fiction *first;* satire, or anything else, second. That was Wells' breakthrough; the beginning of modern science fiction; the lesson we all learned of him, all we later science fiction writers. Nor did Wells rest with his story of time travel. One by one, he developed all the fundamental plots of science fiction and, in every case showed how it ought to be done. Consider the tales of dangerous inventions. It is an old theme. . . . But invisibility? What danger is there in that? . . . In 1897, Wells wrote *The Invisible Man.* . . . From the start, one sees the difficulties of the swathed [covered in bandages] man. What seems like such a gorgeous gift turns out to be nothing of the sort. The difficulties of smoking, of eating, of cold weather, of rain or snow—the story becomes a tragedy. But somehow the tale of dangerous invention does not teach the same lesson in Wells' hands that it does in others'. All the earlier stories of this sort seemed to say 'It is better not to know.' They seem to be hymns to ignorance. Wells, to me, seems to offer the cooler advice of caution. Know, but be careful how you apply. And that, after all, is an important word of advice to us today."

change, Asimov says, science fiction is a constructive and important literary field.

Time and time again, Wells predicted the possible consequences of change and presented them for public reaction. He told people that the future would and should be different and tried to prepare them for it. For that reason, both science fiction writers and readers see Wells as an originator of the field. Writer and literary critic Sam J. Lundwall explains:

Science fiction's strength has always been in its ideas, not in its forms, and the merits of the genre [field] lie not in its . . . [array] of rockets, machines and distant worlds but in the message that nothing, absolutely nothing can be taken for granted, and that we always must be prepared for changes, both in our attitudes and in our environment. . . . When I started to read science fiction seriously . . . it seemed to be offering a subversive thing [something that threatens to overthrow the established order], the prospect of change. . . . [N]o matter what you do, or how much you try to hold back the forces of . . . [nature and humanity], things are going to *change.* Now, the idea of change is deeply subversive to the Establishment, it must always be, and I think this is where H.G. Wells was subversive. . . . What he said was, in effect, that never mind whether it [the future] is going to be better or worse, it is going to be *different.*[75]

An Endless Stream of Ideas

Wells did much more than originate the basic concept and form of science fiction. As mentioned earlier, some of his specific ideas about future inventions inspired the early science fiction writers of the 1920s and 1930s. In the decades that followed, as the genre became more accepted, writers continued to explore Wells' ideas and themes. Isaac Asimov, Arthur C. Clarke, Fritz Leiber, Robert Heinlein, and many other important science fiction writers have expressed their debt to Wells. Asimov called Wells an early master of science fiction, who "laid the groundwork for every theme upon which science fiction writers

have been ringing variations ever since."[76] From Wells' mighty imagination flowed a seemingly endless stream of ideas. In the course of his career, he created or explored nearly every basic science fiction idea, situation, or character, Asimov said. Only a partial list of these includes time travel, journeys to the moon, mad scientists, the destruction of the earth, alien beings, intelligent animals and plants, human extinction, doomsday weapons, computer networks, and extrasensory perception or ESP.

Popular writer Fritz Leiber showed the importance of Wells' influence on other writers by tracing the literary path of just one of Wells' ideas. Leiber chose the time machine concept from the novel of the same name. Said Leiber:

> In his first novel Wells . . . [introduced] many of the visions and techniques

Science fiction writer Robert Heinlein openly acknowledged that Wells greatly influenced him.

[concerning time travel] which appealed to the later science fiction writer. He showed himself less concerned with what might occur next week, and more interested in the happenings of millennia [thousands of years] hence. . . . A brief survey of the . . . treatments of future time travel indicates the pervading influence of Wells. Clifford Simak's *The World of the Red Sun* (1931) . . . John Wyndham's *The Wanderers of Time* (1933) . . . Isaac Asimov's *The End of Eternity* (1955) . . . pursue the Wellsian trail into the distant future.[77]

Wells' ideas and themes are not the only examples of his output that endured. Many of his own writings, now recognized as classics, are still widely read. Tens of thousands of copies of his scientific romances are printed and sold each year by various publishers. These works have been translated into more than seventy languages. It is estimated that more than fifteen million copies of *The War of the Worlds* alone have been printed worldwide in the twentieth century. *The Outline of History,* Wells' most profitable book, also remains in print in the 1990s. In addition, several thousand universities, colleges, and high schools use Wells' scientific romances and utopian books in English literature and science fiction classes. Some schools even have entire courses devoted to the study of Wells and his writings.

Reaching the Masses Through the Media

Wells' impact is not limited to science fiction literature. His works and ideas have also greatly influenced the popular media, including radio and films. One of the most famous examples occurred in 1938, while Wells was still living. American radio personality Orson Welles dramatized H.G. Wells' *The War of the Worlds* in a radio show. As a Halloween prank, Welles structured the show to sound like a series of news bulletins. Thousands of people in New York and New Jersey heard what they believed to be news reports of Martians attacking New York. There was a minor panic that made headlines and turned the amused Orson Welles into a national celebrity overnight. But H.G. Wells was *not* amused. He angrily denounced what he saw as an attempt to use his ideas to terrify people. That had never been his intent.

Filmmakers also eagerly used Wells' books and ideas. He himself saw the movie *Things to Come* as a failure. But long after his death, the film came to be recognized as a classic that was far ahead of its time in

Wells envisioned and depicted many events that would eventually become reality, including space travel to the moon.

Wells' Influence Lives On

Writer Brian Ash, former general secretary of the International H.G. Wells Society, points out that Wells' ideas, works, and influences live on. One way this occurs, says Ash, is that each new generation views the film Wells scripted—Alexander Korda's Things to Come. *The film is now considered a classic, and many of the inventions and events depicted in the film have since become reality. So, Wells' vision lives on to inspire and entertain. Explains Ash in* The Visual Encyclopedia of Science Fiction:

"So much was extraordinary about the flood of baroque, brutal, and often brilliant melodrama of the immediate pre-war [World War II] era, that it appears unjustly overshadowed by the 'great film' of the decade, Alexander Korda's Wells-scripted *Things to Come* (1936), which came near to being a pompous bore in its occasional scenes. That it can retain its fascination, even today, is once more a measure of the elements offered uniquely by science fiction; the baleful prophecy (world war, and the bombing of London), the images of anarchy [chaos] (ruined palaces and casual murder) . . . the visions of progress (flying wings, giant television screens, the space gun) which inevitably present themselves as attainments within our current reach, all the more for having been filmed already. It was an ungainly . . . epic, in keeping with the later writings of Wells, but it remains an epic."

A scene from the now-classic Things to Come. *Wells' film continues to entertain and inspire viewers today.*

Orson Welles (upper left) and cast present a dramatic reading of H.G. Wells'
The War of the Worlds *during a Halloween night radio show in 1938.*
Many listeners believed a Martian invasion was actually happening.

presenting its bold vision of the future. Despite his disappointment with the film, Wells continued to believe that, in films, his ideas would someday reach a far larger audience than they ever could in books. And he was right. Hollywood brought *The War of the Worlds* to the screen in the 1950s and the film won an Oscar for special effects. *The Invisible Man, The First Men in the Moon,* and *The Food of the Gods* became exciting, colorful movies. *The Time Machine* and *The Island of Dr. Moreau* have been filmed several times each. All of these films are available on videotape and remain consistently popular with the public. Such films have introduced H.G. Wells and his explorations of fantastic science to millions of people who have never read one of his books, and they will continue to do so.

Wells even became a character in a movie inspired by his life and work. Director Nicholas Meyer's delightful 1979 film *Time After Time* depicts Wells the writer secretly inventing the time machine he later writes about. Unbeknownst to Wells, one of his friends is Jack the Ripper, who steals the machine and travels to the 1970s. Wells gives chase, and in the process he meets a young woman named Amy Robbins. After disposing of the Ripper, he brings Amy back to his own time and she becomes Jane Wells. For many people, the charming depiction of Wells in the film seemed to transport the great writer from the past into the present.

Freeing Knowledge from the Darkness

Science fiction stories, books, and movies have done more than entertain people. They have made people aware of the possibilities of science. They have also made people believe that whatever can be

Invading Martian spaceships devastate earth in the 1953 Academy Award-winning film version of Wells' The War of the Worlds.

A movie poster advertises the film adaptation of Wells' novel.

Claude Rains and Gloria Stuart starred in the popular film version of Wells' The Invisible Man.

Mutants carry off the body of their human keeper in the 1977 film The Island of Dr. Moreau, *based on Wells' novel.*

In The Time Machine, *actor Rod Taylor, as Wells' Time Traveler, sets the controls of his time machine for the distant future.*

Malcolm McDowell played H.G. Wells in the 1979 film fantasy Time After Time. *In it, Wells actually invents the time machine he only wrote about in real life. The Wells character is shown here in his time machine.*

imagined can be accomplished. Writer Arthur C. Clarke described communications satellites in a story in the 1940s. These devices later became a reality, partly because

In the 1940s, renowned science fiction author Arthur C. Clarke wrote about communications satellites. Inspired by Clarke's stories, scientists later made such satellites reality.

the story inspired some of the young people who read it to become space scientists.

Similarly, Wells' own predictions about atomic energy, computers, and space travel helped make these things realities. In fact, so many of Wells' prophecies came true after his death that people began to see that he was much more than a mere entertainer. The name H.G. Wells became synonymous with the machines and ideas of the future. His unknowing contribution to science fiction helped influence generations of young people to become scientists.

As Wells so correctly pointed out, the goal of scientists is to unlock the mysteries of nature. They seek that knowledge Wells described—the knowledge that is hidden in the darkness just beyond the flame of the lit match. By helping make advanced science a reality, H.G. Wells freed some of that knowledge from the darkness. And in so doing, he made society better. Therefore, though he did not live to see it, he achieved his goal of helping to build a better world after all.

Notes

Chapter 1: Escape from Childhood

1. H.G. Wells, *Experiment in Autobiography: Discoveries and Conclusions of a Very Ordinary Brain*. London: Cresset Press, 1934.

2. Lovat Dickson, *H.G. Wells: His Turbulent Life and Times*. New York: Atheneum, 1969.

3. From *The Diary of Sarah Wells*. H.G. Wells Archive, Urbana: University of Illinois.

4. Wells, *Experiment*.

5. Dickson, *H.G. Wells*.

6. Wells, *Experiment*.

7. Norman Mackenzie and Jeanne Mackenzie, *The Time Traveller: The Life of H.G. Wells*. London: Weidenfeld and Nicolson, 1973.

8. Reproduced in Wells, *Experiment*.

9. Mackenzie and Mackenzie, *The Time Traveller*.

10. Wells, *Experiment*.

11. H.G. Wells, "The Man of the Year Million," in *Certain Personal Matters*, London: Lawrence and Bullen, 1897.

Chapter 2: Travels in Time

12. Letter to A.T. Simmons, August 1887, Wells Archive.

13. Letter to A.T. Simmons, December 1887, Wells Archive.

14. Letter to Morley Davies, December 1887, Wells Archive.

15. Letter from T. Ormerod to the *Manchester Guardian*, August 21, 1946.

16. H.G. Wells, "The Rediscovery of the Unique," *Fortnightly Review*, July 1891.

17. Wells, *Experiment*.

18. Wells, *Experiment*.

19. W.T. Stead, *Review of Reviews*, March 1895.

20. H.G. Wells, *The Time Machine*, 1895.

21. Wells, *The Time Machine*.

22. Dickson, *H.G. Wells*.

Chapter 3: The Scientific Romances

23. MacKenzie and Mackenzie, *The Time Traveller*.

24. Letter to Elizabeth Healy, 1896, Wells Archive.

25. H.G. Wells, *The War of the Worlds*, 1898.

26. Wells, *The War of the Worlds*.

27. Wells, *The War of the Worlds*.

28. Letter from Wells to his parents, February 5, 1895, Wells Archive.

29. H.G. Wells, *The Invisible Man*, 1897.

30. Letter to Wells from Joseph Conrad, 1897, Wells Archive.

31. Letter to Arnold Bennett, summer 1901, Wells Archive.

Chapter 4: A Gift of Prophecy

32. H.G. Wells, printed in *Nature*, February 6, 1902.

33. Wells, *Experiment*.

34. Wilson Harris, *Arnold Bennett and H.G. Wells*. London: Faber and Faber, 1960.

35. H.G. Wells, *Anticipations of the Reaction of Mechanical and Scientific Progress upon Human Life and Thought*, 1901.

36. Quoted in Ford Madox Ford, *Mightier than the Sword*. London: Allen and Unwin, 1938.

37. Wells, *Anticipations*.

38. Wells, *Anticipations*.

39. Dickson, *H.G. Wells*.

40. Letter from Wells to Frederick Macmillan, August 9, 1905, Wells Archive.

41. Letter to Wells from Henry James, November 19, 1905, in Leon Edel and Gordon N. Ray, *Henry James and H.G. Wells.* London: Harper & Row, 1958.

42. Letter to Haden Guest, December 12, 1905, Wells Archive.

43. Wells, *Experiment.*

Chapter 5: Stirring Up Controversy

44. Letter to H.G. Wells from Jane Wells, 1903, Wells Archive.

45. Letter to H.G. Wells from Jane Wells, April 26, 1906, Wells Archive.

46. Dickson, *H.G. Wells.*

47. Wells, *Experiment.*

48. Letter to Wells from Frederick Macmillan, October 19, 1909, Wells Archive.

49. *Spectator,* November 1909.

50. *Spectator,* December 1909.

51. H.G. Wells, *Ann Veronica,* 1909.

Chapter 6: Toward a New World Order

52. Letter to Henry James, July 6, 1910, in Edel and Ray, *Henry James and H.G. Wells.*

53. Mackenzie and Mackenzie, *The Time Traveller.*

54. H.G. Wells, *Joan and Peter,* 1918, preface to 1927 edition.

55. Leo Szilard, *Collected Works.* Cambridge, MA: MIT Press, 1972.

56. H.G. Wells, *The World Set Free.*

57. H.G. Wells, *Men Like Gods,* 1923.

Chapter 7: History as Teacher

58. Dickson, *H.G. Wells.*

59. Mackenzie and Mackenzie, *The Time Traveller.*

60. Printed in *Today and Tomorrow,* September/October 1920.

61. Letter to Wells from Arnold Bennett, January 22, 1920, in Harris, *Arnold Bennett and H.G. Wells.*

62. Arnold Toynbee, *A Study of History,* Vol. 1. London: Oxford University Press, 1934.

63. H.G. Wells, *The Outline of History.* New York: Doubleday, 1920.

64. Letter to Jane Wells, May 10, 1927, Wells Archive.

65. Janet Dunbar, *Mrs. G.B.S.* New York: Harper & Row, 1963.

Chapter 8: The Eternal Optimist

66. H.G. Wells, from a speech, "The Informative Content of Education," to the British Association, 1937, quoted in Mackenzie and Mackenzie, *The Time Traveller.*

67. Mackenzie and Mackenzie, *The Time Traveller.*

68. Letter to Wells from Franklin D. Roosevelt, February 13, 1935, Wells Archive.

69. Letter to Arthur Bliss, June 29, 1934, printed in Arthur Bliss, *As I Remember.* London: Faber, 1970.

70. H.G. Wells, film script for *Things to Come,* 1935.

71. From Beatrice Webb's diary, March 31, 1939.

72. Letter to *British Weekly,* June 26, 1939.

Chapter 9: A Mighty Imagination

73. Letter to Wilson Harris, 1938. Wells Archive.

74. Isaac Asimov, "Escape into Reality," *The Humanist,* November/December 1957.

75. Sam J. Lundwall, *Science Fiction: What It's All About.* New York: Ace Books, 1971.

76. Asimov, "Escape into Reality."

77. Fritz Leiber, "Time and the Nth Dimensions," in Brian Ash, ed., *The Visual Encyclopedia of Science Fiction.* New York: Harmony Books, 1977.

For Further Reading

Author's note: All of the following works by and about H.G. Wells are entertaining, informative, and worthwhile. Most are available at public libraries. If your library does not have the one you are looking for, ask the librarian if it is possible to borrow it from a neighboring library.

Books about Wells

Brian Ash, editor, *The Visual Encyclopedia of Science Fiction*. New York: Harmony Books, 1977. Contains dozens of references to Wells and his works, mainly his short stories, scientific romances, and utopian books. Analyzes how these works have influenced the course of science fiction.

Alan L. Paley, *H.G. Wells: Author of Famous Science Fiction Stories*. Charlotteville, NY: SamHar Press, 1972. A good general synopsis of Wells and his major works.

by Wells

The following works by H.G. Wells are available in a number of different editions. Since any edition is suitable, the author does not cite a particular edition.

The Time Machine is Wells' first important work. A colorful, fascinating story that has inspired several films. The idea that humans might destroy their own civilization seems even more believable in today's world of pollution and atomic energy than it was in Wells' day. This makes the book even more compelling than when it was written.

The War of the Worlds is perhaps the finest depiction of an invasion of the earth ever written. The scenes of the Martians destroying the countryside with heat rays and the narrator trapped in a ruined house by the invaders are riveting and unforgettable.

The World Set Free is a bit difficult to read but is fascinating and worthwhile. One of the best examples of Wells preaching about how to better the world, while predicting the marvels and ills of the future. Atomic energy and bombs are only some of the things he discusses.

"The Crystal Egg" is a fascinating tale of a strange artifact found in an antique store that turns out to be a device that can communicate with a bizarre Martian civilization.

"The Empire of the Ants" suggests that ants might evolve intelligence like humans did. But will the ants want to share the world with people?

"The Sea Raiders" is a strange story of unknown creatures rising from the ocean depths to threaten humans.

"The Star" is one of Wells' best short stories, about a star from outside the solar system on a collision course with earth. Contains vivid descriptions of earthquakes, tidal waves, and other disasters.

"The Stolen Bacillus" focuses on a terrorist who tries to poison the public water supply with deadly germs. Has an interesting twist ending.

Things to Come. In 1935, Wells wrote the script for this imaginative movie about humanity rising from the ashes of a world war and building a modern space-faring society. Wells' personal ideas and philosophy ring out clearly in the dialogue. The special effects and futuristic sets were state-of-the-art at the time and still look fairly believable. Available at many video stores.

Works Consulted

Alfred Borrello, *H.G. Wells: Author in Agony.* Champaign, IL: University of Illinois Press, 1972. A good general synopsis of Wells' life, emphasizing his frustrations and disappointments at not achieving his main goal, namely to bring about significant social changes in his own lifetime.

Basil Davenport, editor, *The Science Fiction Novel: Imagination and Social Criticism.* Chicago: Advent, 1964. Various writers analyze the structure, worth, and impact of science fiction novels, including those of Wells. His work is seen as a precursor that influenced the science fiction genre.

Lovat Dickson, *H.G. Wells: His Turbulent Life and Times.* New York: Atheneum, 1969. A scholarly biography of Wells that deals less with the smaller details of his life and more with how his attitudes and feelings about life tended to come out strongly in his writings. Includes many quotes from his works and letters, and also from letters to him from family, friends, and associates.

Mark R. Hillegas, *The Future as Nightmare: H.G. Wells & the Anti-Utopians.* Champaign, IL: University of Illinois Press, 1974. Here, Wells is seen as one of several writers who created in their works future societies with negative or frightening aspects. These anti-utopias, the opposite of ideal societies, are discussed as literary reactions to the sudden social, political, and scientific changes of the twentieth century.

John Huntington, *The Logic of Fantasy: H.G. Wells & Science Fiction.* New York: Columbia University Press, 1982. An overall view of how Wells' own unique brand of fantastic literature became a major cornerstone of the science fiction genre.

Sam J. Lundwall, *Science Fiction: What It's All About.* New York: Ace Books, 1971. This general overview of science fiction literature discusses and describes the importance of several of Wells' works, particularly *The Time Machine, The War of the Worlds, The Shape of Things to Come, The Island of Dr. Moreau,* and *The World Set Free.*

Norman and Jeanne Mackenzie, *The Time Traveller: The Life of H.G. Wells.* London: Weidenfeld and Nicolson, 1973. An excellent biography of Wells. Very detailed and scholarly, including numerous quotes from Wells' books, articles, speeches, letters, as well as remarks about him by friends, publishers, and critics. Sometimes difficult reading but perhaps the most thorough analysis available of Wells' life.

H.G. Wells, *Experiment in Autobiography: Discoveries and Conclusions of a Very Ordinary Man.* London: Cresset Press, 1934. Fascinating, although sometimes ponderous, reading. Wells recounts the highlights of his own life up until 1934.

H.G. Wells, *The Outline of History.* New York: Doubleday, 1920. More than seventy years after its publication, this remains a brilliant overview of world history. Occasionally, new editions are printed, in which the editors provide updates that take into account research and discoveries made since Wells' death. Wells' writing style and vocabulary are, in places, a bit difficult for modern audiences, but it is still very worthwhile reading.

Index

Picture Credits

Cover Photo: FPG, Inc.

AP/Wide World Photos, 65, 69, 77 (bottom), 85 (top), 89, 91

The Bettmann Archive, 14 (bottom), 37 (bottom), 38 (bottom), 52 (top), 54, 57, 74, 79, 88

Bettmann/Hulton, 11, 17, 18, 30 (bottom), 45

Brown Brothers, 30 (top), 48, 53 (top), 61

Culver Pictures, 10 (top), 63

Franklin D. Roosevelt Library, 84

Hollywood Book and Poster, 35, 93, 95 (all), 96 (both), 97 (top)

Hulton Deutsch Collection, 52 (bottom), 53 (bottom), 56, 60, 82, 86

The Library of Congress, 14 (top), 21, 77 (top)

Los Alamos National Laboratory, 67

National Archives, 71

NASA, 92

San Francisco Academy of Comic Art, 34 (both), 38 (top), 39, 66

Smithsonian, 49, 68

Topham, 19 (bottom), 36, 46, 73

University Of Illinois Library at Urbana-Champaign, 9, 10 (bottom), 12, 13, 15, 19 (top), 22, 23, 25 (both), 27 (both), 33, 43 (all), 44, 58, 76, 81, 85 (bottom)

UPI/Bettmann, 37 (top), 97 (bottom)

UPI/Bettmann Newsphotos, 94

About the Author

Don Nardo is an award-winning writer. Mr. Nardo's writing credits include short stories, articles, and more than thirty-five books, including *Lasers, Gravity, Oil Spills, Anxiety and Phobias, The Irish Potato Famine, Exercise, The Mexican-American War, The Persian Gulf War, Animation, Medical Diagnosis,* and the biographies *Charles Darwin* and *Joseph Smith.* Among his other writings are an episode of ABC's *Spenser: for Hire* and numerous screenplays. Mr. Nardo lives with his wife Christine on Cape Cod, Massachusetts.